Praise for Teacher Moves

"Shannon perfectly captures the heart and art of great teaching."

—Mario Spagnuolo, President, Greater Essex County Elementary Teachers' Local & Executive Member, Elementary Teachers' Federation of Ontario

"*Teacher Moves* is the perfect balance of real-world advice and inspiration. Shannon reminds us that great teaching isn't about doing more—it's about doing what matters most."

—Kris Marentette, Principal

Teacher Moves is packed with strategies that make a tangible difference in classrooms. These strategies don't just help students thrive, they help teachers feel more confident, effective, and energized. If you want a classroom where everyone can flourish, this book is your guide.

—Lynn McLaughlin, Former Superintendent of Education

"This book is an incredible resource for new teachers. It shows that great teaching isn't just about academics—it's about nurturing students' social and emotional growth as well. Shannon reminds us of what it truly means to be an effective, caring teacher."

—Andrea Maziak, Teacher & Founder of Crushing Limits Education Co

"Clear, doable strategies that actually work."

—Kyle Matthews, Teacher

"This book gave me the confidence to stop overcomplicating my teaching. The moves are straightforward, effective, and truly make students feel seen and supported."

—Julie Power, First-Year Teacher

"I've been teaching for over twenty years, and I still found fresh ideas and reminders in these pages. This is not just for new teachers—veterans will walk away reinspired."

—Sandra Fields, 25-Year Teaching Veteran

TEACHER MOVES

Published by teacherEDU

Book Cover and Interior Layout by Melissa Williams Design

Photography by Heike Delmore

First Edition

ISBN: 978-1-7382593-2-8 (paperback)
ISBN: 978-1-7382593-3-5 (eBook)

WHAT GREAT TEACHERS DO

TEACHER MOVES

98 HIGH-IMPACT STRATEGIES FOR BETTER TEACHING AND LEARNING OUTCOMES

SHANNON HAZEL

Contents

Author's Note ix
Definition xi
Introduction xiii

Chapter 1: Teacher Moves 1
Chapter 2 : Classroom Management Moves 9
Chapter 3: Instructional Moves 49
Chapter 4: Relationship-Building Moves 91
Chapter 5: Engagement Moves 129
Chapter 6: Differentiation Moves 165
Chapter 7: Adaptive Moves 209
Chapter 8: Emotional Support Moves 235
Chapter 9: Reflective Moves 273
Chapter 10: Laying the Foundation 299

Quick Reference Guide 309
About the Author 313
Also by Shannon Hazel 314

Author's Note

The strategies in this book—what I call "teacher moves"—represent a collection of high-impact actions teachers use to support student learning, classroom management, and professional growth. While I've worked hard to organize these moves into clear categories (such as instructional, engagement, or emotional support), I want to acknowledge that this list is not exhaustive, and the categories are not rigid.

Many moves naturally overlap. A strategy that boosts engagement might also support classroom management. A reflective move might lead to an instructional shift. Teaching is dynamic, and the impact of any move often depends on the context, the students, and the moment.

The categories presented here reflect the most common use or intention of each move, based on my experience and professional judgment. They are meant to guide—not limit—your thinking and practice.

My hope is that this book sparks reflection, experimentation, and continued growth as you develop your own toolkit of teacher moves.

Definition

teacher moves *plural noun*

1. The deliberate actions, strategies, or decisions teachers make to promote learning, manage classroom dynamics, and meet student needs. Often subtle yet powerful, teacher moves may occur spontaneously in response to classroom situations or be embedded in planned instruction. Rooted in pedagogical knowledge and professional experience, these moves aim to create an engaging, responsive, and effective learning environment.

Introduction

Have you ever walked into a classroom and instantly felt the vibe?

Maybe the energy was calm, focused, and welcoming—you could tell students knew what to do and felt good about being there. Or maybe it was the opposite: loud, off-task, and chaotic, with tension hanging in the air.

If you've worked as a supply teacher, prep provider, or rotary teacher, you know exactly what that moment feels like. Within seconds, you're scanning the room—reading the interactions, checking the physical setup, and figuring out how to enter the space as the new adult in the room.

And just like that, you get a gut sense of how the day might go.

So, what makes the difference?

Why do some classrooms run like well-oiled machines while others feel like you're constantly putting out fires? Why do some spaces feel calm and student-centered while others feel out of control?

Here's the truth: it's not just about the students, the school, or the seating chart. It's about the *moves* the teacher makes.

In this book, we'll focus on one powerful, often overlooked ingredient of successful classrooms: the intentional, strategic choices teachers make in the moment—what we'll call *teacher moves*. We'll explore eight categories of moves that, when used thoughtfully, can transform your teaching and your classroom culture.

By the end of this book, you'll:

- Understand the eight types of teacher moves—and when and why to use them.
- Learn what makes these moves effective and how to apply them in real time.
- Discover the foundational elements that support effective classroom management.
- Gain practical, doable strategies you can use right away.

Whether you're new to the classroom or decades in, mastering your teacher moves isn't just about making your life easier (though it *will*). It's about creating a space where students feel safe, supported, and ready to learn.

Let's dive in.

Chapter 1
Teacher Moves

Great teachers lead with empathy, teach with intention, and grow with reflection.

You walk into your classroom with your lesson planned, your whiteboard already prepped, and your materials ready to go. Today's goal: help your grade 3 students understand the concept of arrays in multiplication. You're excited—it's a lesson you enjoy teaching, and you've even brought in some colored stickers to make it hands-on.

The first few minutes go smoothly. You're modeling how to arrange stickers in neat rows and columns. "Three rows of four," you say, tapping out each group slowly. "Let's count together!" The students chant, "3, 6, 9, 12," and you nod. Great start.

But then—you notice movement. Khalen and Betty are whispering behind their math notebooks. Keisha, who usually loves math, is staring out the window. And Marcus? He's stuck, confused by the array worksheet you handed out and trying to copy from the student next to him.

So, what do you do?

You take a few quiet steps closer to Khalen and Betty—**proximity move**—and their whispering stops. That's a simple classroom management move. You catch Keisha's eye and call her name warmly to invite her to help you model the next problem on the board—**an engagement move.** As for Marcus, you kneel beside him, simplify the directions with a quick sketch and verbal explanation—**an adaptive move**—and ask him to try the next one with you. Then, you hand him a version of the worksheet with fewer questions, knowing he needs more processing time—**a differentiation move.**

None of this was in your lesson plan.

And yet—you're teaching. You're doing more than that. You're orchestrating the learning experience with intention and responsiveness. These are teacher moves.

What Is a Teacher Move?

Teacher moves are the small but powerful decisions you make—sometimes planned, sometimes in the moment—that help keep learning on track, students engaged, and the classroom running smoothly. Think of them as your toolkit. The more experience you gain, the more tools you collect—and the more confidence you'll have about which one to use, when.

Ultimately, teacher moves are about connection—connecting with students, connecting students with content, and connecting teaching strategies to learning outcomes.

Not all teacher moves look dramatic. Most are subtle. A pause before asking a question. A hand on a student's desk to re-center their attention. A shift in tone. A regrouping of students when energy dips. These things may not seem like much, but they're what experienced teachers rely on to adjust and respond to the messy, wonderful, sometimes unpredictable, reality of today's classrooms.

The Power of Teacher Moves

When I was in Grade 8, French class was... painful. We dreaded it. We weren't interested. We weren't engaged and we certainly weren't cooperative. Most days, we spent more time trying to derail the lesson than learn the language. One student made it his mission to shut the class down entirely—and most of us let him.

Then something unexpected happened.

One Friday afternoon, our ***former*** French teacher—the one who taught us in Grades 4 through 6—walked into the room for a surprise visit. The vibe shifted immediately. The energy lifted. Every single student smiled. We cheered. We begged him to teach us something.

He agreed, picked a topic on the spot, and within minutes we were all participating, laughing, and—without even realizing it—learning French again.

I've thought about that moment many times, now as an adult and as an educator.

What changed?

It wasn't the language. It wasn't the content. It wasn't even us.

It was ***him***.

We respected him. We trusted him. We felt safe and seen with him. He had built relationships with us years earlier—and somehow, in that one visit, those old connections still held strong.

I look back now not just with regret for how we treated our Grade 8 French teacher, but with insight into why it happened. That moment reminded me that students respond to more than just a lesson plan—they respond to the ***person*** delivering it. The vibe, the tone, the relationship, the consistency, the belief that they matter.

That shift in energy. That was the power of teacher moves at work. Let's look at the types of moves you'll learn about in this book.

Types of Moves

Teacher moves fall into several key categories—each serving a specific purpose in the classroom. You'll find yourself using a blend of these moves throughout your day.

In this book, we'll explore eight categories of teacher moves.

Type of Move	Purpose
Classroom Management Moves	Keep things focused, orderly, and safe.
Instructional Moves	Guide student learning.
Relationship-Building Moves	Strengthen trust and connection with students.
Engagement Moves	Spark curiosity and increase participation.
Differentiation Moves	Meet students where they're at and move them forward.
Adaptive Moves	Pivots when students are confused, restless, or need a shift.
Emotional Support Moves	Foster social-emotional well-being and learning readiness.
Reflective Moves	These are for you—they help you grow and build confidence over time.

Why These Moves Matter

Teaching isn't just about covering the curriculum—it's about crafting a space where learning feels possible, purposeful, and personal. The right teacher moves help you do just that.

They help:

- Keep students engaged and focused on learning.
- Support diverse learning styles and needs.
- Reduce disruptions while maximizing meaningful learning time.
- Build strong relationships that motivate students to show up and try.
- Continuously grow your teaching practice—so every day feels more intentional than the last.

Every move you make shapes the learning environment —and how students see themselves in it.

What Makes a Teacher Move Effective?

Some teacher moves shift the energy of the room in an instant. Others take time to build their impact. So, what makes some moves so powerful and others less effective?

The best teacher moves aren't complicated or flashy. They're rooted in clarity, purpose, and strong teaching instincts. When you choose moves with intention and use them consistently, you build trust, momentum, and a culture where learning can thrive.

Here's what effective teacher moves have in common:

They're Intentional

Great teacher moves serve a clear purpose—whether it's clarifying a tough concept, easing a tense moment, or bringing focus back to the room. You don't just react. You respond with purpose.

They're Responsive

No two days (or students) are exactly alike. The most effective moves allow for flexibility. You notice when something's not landing—and you shift, whether that means rewording directions, regrouping students, or changing the pace.

They're Grounded in Strong Practice

High-impact moves come from experience, reflection, and sound pedagogy. They're supported by what we know works—developmentally appropriate practices, relationship-based teaching, and real-time observation.

They're Clear and Consistent

Students thrive when they know what to expect. When your moves are predictable, clearly communicated, and used with consistency, students feel more secure and are more likely to engage, take risks, and self-regulate.

The most effective moves are thoughtful, responsive, and rooted in what matters most—your students.

When you teach with intention, stay attuned to your students, and ground your actions in good practice, you create a classroom where both you and your students can succeed.

How Do You Know Which Moves to Use?

There's no one-size-fits-all strategy when it comes to teaching. What works for one teacher—or even one class—might not work for another. That's why the best approach is to build a toolkit of moves that fit your teaching style, meet your students' needs, and work in your specific environment.

Here's how to start building that toolkit with purpose:

1. Reflect on Your Teaching Style

Ask yourself:

- Do I prefer structure or spontaneity?
- Am I more proactive or reactive?
- Do I rely on energy and presence or on calm and consistency?

Let your natural strengths guide your strategy selection.

2. Assess Your Classroom

What patterns do you notice?

- Are students disengaged?
- Are transitions rocky?
- Are academic needs wide-ranging?

3. Try It, Watch, Adjust

Don't wait for the perfect moment or perfect plan. Choose one move. Use it consistently. Watch how your students respond. Then reflect and adjust.

4. Get Feedback

Talk to a trusted colleague. Ask students what helps them focus or feel supported. You'll gain insight—and new ideas.

5. Reflect Often

After a lesson or a challenging moment, pause and ask:

- What worked well here?
- What didn't land the way I expected?
- What might I try differently next time?

This habit of reflection helps you sharpen your instincts and grow your toolkit over time.

Building Your Toolkit

Building your collection of teacher moves isn't about mastering a rigid list—it's about growing your instincts, sharpening your awareness, and staying connected to your students. It's part art, part science, and always a work in progress.

Some moves will become go-to favorites. Others might evolve—or get replaced—as your students change and your teaching grows. That's the beauty of a flexible toolkit: it grows with you.

Each intentional move you make adds to your capacity to teach with clarity, compassion, and confidence.

The best teacher moves often go unnoticed—except by the students who needed them most.

The Bottom Line

You don't need to have all the answers or master every category of teacher moves right away. But the more intentional and responsive you become in how you manage your lessons, relationships, and classroom environment, the more confident—and effective—you'll be.

Every smooth transition, every re-engaged student, every moment of clarity during a lesson—they all start with a thoughtful move made by you.

You've already made great moves. You'll make more tomorrow. Keep growing your toolkit, one move at a time.

Up Next

In the following chapters, we will take a deep dive into eight different types of teacher moves. First, we'll start with the foundation: creating a classroom environment where learning can happen.

Classroom management moves are the quiet engines that keep everything running—helping you set expectations, maintain focus, and create a space where students feel safe, respected, and ready to learn.

In the next chapter, we'll look at practical, high-impact strategies you can use to keep your classroom calm, productive, and primed for meaningful learning.

Chapter 2

Classroom Management Moves

"My teacher doesn't yell. She just gives you that look, and somehow, you stop." —**Grade 4 student**

Let's be real—you can have the most engaging lesson plan, with beautiful visuals, hands-on materials, and creative activities. But if the classroom isn't calm and focused, it's tough for real learning to happen.

Classroom management isn't about control. It's about creating a space where students feel safe, supported, and ready to learn. It's what allows teaching to take root and learning to take off.

It doesn't require being strict or raising your voice—you just need to be clear, consistent, and intentional.

In this chapter, you'll learn practical, effective classroom management strategies you can start using right away. You'll see how small, intentional actions can help your day flow more smoothly, your students feel more secure, and your lessons land the way you intended.

Why These Moves Matter

Classroom management is the foundation of teaching and learning. When expectations are clear, routines are smooth, and the environment is calm, students can focus. And so can you.

Strong classroom management moves help you:

- Optimize learning time.
- Reduce stress—for you and your students.
- Build a culture of respect and shared responsibility.

- Minimize disruptions and keep learning flowing.
- Create a sense of safety that supports emotional regulation.

Classroom management isn't about fixing behavior —it's about shaping a culture.

So, What Are Classroom Management Moves?

Classroom management moves are the small, intentional actions you take to guide the tone, flow, and behavior in your classroom. Some are proactive—like posting the daily schedule or teaching a transition routine. Others are responsive—like moving closer to a student who's off-task or using a quiet cue to bring the group back together.

They don't require re-inventing the wheel or hours of planning. They just require clarity, consistency, and care.

When used well, classroom management moves help your classroom feel organized, respectful, and calm—even on the wildest days.

What You Notice Grows

After twenty-five years in the classroom, I've experimented with countless classroom management strategies. But one move that has stayed with me through every grade and setting is positive narration.

It's simple. It's subtle. And it works.

Instead of calling out off-task behavior, I shout out who's on track:

"I see Jordan has his notebook open and is getting started."

"Love how Maya is using her quiet voice to check in with her partner."

"Octavia looks ready to learn!"

This small shift in attention sends a powerful message: I see you. I value your effort. I believe in who you're becoming.

And the ripple effect? Students notice—and follow suit. They want that positive attention. They want to be seen doing the right thing.

This strategy doesn't require volume or fanfare. It just requires presence, awareness, and an intention to give energy to what's working. And over time, it helps shape your community of learners.

Why These Moves Work?

Classroom management moves aren't just about keeping order—they're about shaping a classroom where learning feels possible, predictable, and safe. At their core, these moves help you prepare for success and respond calmly when things go sideways.

Here's what strong classroom management moves do:

Promote Positive Behavior

Students want to be seen doing the right thing. When you name what's working—like through positive narration or structured choice—students rise to meet your expectations.

Minimize Disruptions

Off-task behavior is part of teaching. Effective management moves—like quiet redirection, proximity, or a nonverbal cue—keep things on track without turning small issues into big ones.

Keep Learning Moving

A well-managed classroom isn't silent. It's active and focused. Clear routines, structured transitions, and posted expectations help students stay focused and self-directed—so the momentum keeps going.

Create a Safe Environment

Classrooms run best when students feel safe, both physically and emotionally. Greeting students by name, using calm tones, and responding with empathy all build that safety.

In addition, the most effective classroom management strategies are:

- **Proactive** – You prevent problems before they start.
- **Responsive** – You address what's happening in the moment.
- **Consistent** – Students know what to expect from you.
- **Supportive** – You maintain boundaries with care, not control.

Classroom management is not about control—it's about buy-in.

Real Talk: What This Looks Like in Action

It's Tuesday afternoon. You're halfway through a math lesson. Two students are whispering, one is daydreaming, and the energy is slipping.

What do you do?

- Step closer to the whisperers without saying a word—***proximity move.***
- Pause and scan the room to regain attention—***nonverbal cue.***
- Switch up the activity to include movement—***responsive move.***
- Narrate what's working: "Thanks to Table 2 for resetting so quickly."—***positive narration move.***

That whole reset takes under two minutes—but it shifts the tone. That's the power of intentional classroom management moves.

They're small, but they're mighty.

You Don't Have to Do It All at Once

No teacher will master classroom management overnight. Start with a few key moves that fit your style and your students' needs.

You might begin with:

- Teaching and practicing an entry routine.
- Using a quiet signal to bring attention back.
- Narrating positive behavior throughout the day.
- Posting a visual schedule to support transitions.

Observe. Adjust. Reflect. Stay curious. The more you practice, the more natural it becomes.

Classroom management is an art that gets better with time, experience, and patience—with your students *and* yourself.

Let's Explore: 14 Classroom Management Moves

On the following pages, we'll take a closer look at fourteen moves you can use to foster a calm, structured, and learning-focused classroom environment:

Structured Routines
Daily Schedule
Strategic Seating
The Proximity Effect
Nonverbal Cues
Attention Signals
Name-Dropping
Positive Narration
Wait-and-Redirect
Noise Level Chart
Structured Choice
Front-Loading Expectations
Transition Timers
Movement Breaks

Let's take a closer look at each.

Structured Routines

Purpose:

To improve the daily flow of the classroom and maximize learning time.

Description:

This strategy involves creating consistent patterns and procedures that guide how the classroom operates. Structured routines help students know what to expect, reduce transition time, and create a calm, predictable environment. By minimizing uncertainty, you free up more energy for learning and keep the focus on instruction instead of logistics.

How to Use It:

1. Teach Routines Explicitly

Model and practice routines just like you teach academic skills. Show students how to enter the classroom, transition between tasks, or get materials.

2. Be Consistent

Follow the routine the same way each time so students internalize the flow.

3. Adjust as Needed

If something isn't working, tweak the routine with input from your students.

Example: At the start of each day, you guide students through a consistent arrival routine: they hang up backpacks, place homework in a bin, and begin a morning warm-up activity posted on the whiteboard. Because the routine becomes automatic, your students settle quickly, reducing off-task behavior and allowing the day to start calmly.

When to Use It:

- At the beginning of the year to establish classroom culture
- For daily entry, dismissal, and transition points
- When you want to build student independence
- All day, every day

Why It Works:

✓ Students know what to expect and how things work

✓ Reduces anxiety, limits disruptions, and maximizes learning time

✓ Builds a smooth rhythm that supports focus

Daily Schedule

Purpose:

To help students understand the flow of the day, reduce uncertainty, and promote time management.

Description:

This strategy involves posting a clear, age-appropriate outline of the day's events so students know what to expect and when. A visible daily schedule reduces uncertainty, supports time management, and helps students transition smoothly between activities with confidence.

How to Use It:

1. Post the Schedule Where Everyone Can See It

Write the day's activities on the board, use a pocket chart, or display it digitally so that students can see it throughout the day. Include subjects, transitions, and special events.

2. Keep It Clear and Concise

Use consistent language and format. For younger students, pair words with visuals or icons to support understanding.

3. Review the Schedule Together

Start the day by walking through the schedule so students know what to expect. Mention any changes or surprises upfront to avoid confusion later and prepare students who struggle with change.

4. Make Updates Transparent

If plans change, update the schedule in front of students and explain why. This models flexibility while maintaining trust and routine.

Example: In your classroom, you write the daily schedule on the whiteboard each morning. After recess, when a student asks, "Are we still doing art today?" you point to the schedule and say, "Let's check!" Then you review the remainder of the day—highlighting when art will take place.

When to Use It:

- At the start of each school day
- During transitions and unexpected changes
- To reduce anxiety or for answering time-related questions

Why It Works:

✓ Helps students mentally prepare for what's next

✓ Reduces uncertainty and questions

✓ Builds independence and time management skills

Strategic Seating

Purpose:

To reduce distractions and support student focus and collaboration.

Description:

This strategy involves intentionally arranging where students sit to minimize distractions, improve focus, and encourage positive peer interactions. The goal is not to punish students but to create an environment where everyone can engage and learn successfully.

How to Use It:

1. Observe Student Dynamics

Notice who works well together, who needs fewer distractions, and who may benefit from proximity to you.

2. Assign Seats with Purpose

Place students where they are most likely to succeed—this could mean separating easily distracted peers, pairing students for peer support, or creating mixed-ability groups for collaboration.

3. Be Flexible

Change seating arrangements as needed based on behavior patterns, academic needs, or shifting classroom dynamics. Try rows, groups, pairs, or U-shapes. Let purpose guide your layout.

4. Communicate Expectations

Explain that strategic seating is about setting everyone up for success, not punishment—it is to help everyone learn better.

Example: You notice that one student stays more focused when seated near the front of the room. At the next transition, you invite them to move to a spot closer to you and the board. With this small shift, the student follows directions more easily and participates with greater confidence.

When to Use It:

- At the start of a term, unit or after a break in the school year
- When focus or peer dynamics shift
- To support collaboration or individual needs

Why It Works:

✓ Reduces off-task behavior and friction

✓ Boosts engagement through smart pairings

✓ Shows students you're paying attention to what helps them learn

The Proximity Effect

Purpose:

To gently redirect behavior without interrupting instruction.

Description:

This strategy involves moving closer to students to subtly redirect behavior, refocus attention, or prevent issues from escalating. Proximity provides a quiet, nonconfrontational way to support students while keeping the flow of instruction uninterrupted.

How to Use It:

1. **Notice Off-Task Behavior**

   Watch for students who are distracted, chatting, or not following directions.

2. **Move with Purpose**

   Continue teaching, monitoring the room, or giving directions as you calmly walk toward the student or group.

3. **Convey Presence**

   Stand nearby without singling anyone out or making direct eye contact. Your calm presence signals that you are aware and attentive.

4. **Return to Neutral**

   When the behavior improves, move away naturally to reinforce the positive behavior without drawing attention.

Example: During group work, a student begins whispering off-topic to a peer. You continue circulating, calmly stepping closer to the group, and the student quickly refocuses without you needing to say a word.

When to Use It:

- During direct instruction, independent work, or group work
- When you spot early signs of distraction
- As a first response to off-task behavior

Why It Works:

✓ Quietly diffuses misbehavior without public correction

✓ Keeps instruction flowing

✓ Reinforces teacher awareness and presence

Nonverbal Cues

Purpose:

To guide behavior quickly and quietly.

Description:

This strategy involves using silent signals—such as gestures, hand motions, or facial expressions—to communicate directions, reminders, or redirections. Nonverbal cues allow you to manage behavior and guide students without interrupting the flow of instruction.

How to Use It:

1. Teach the Signals

Introduce nonverbal signals at the beginning of the year or before starting a new routine. Model each gesture and explain what it means. For example, holding up one finger might signal a bathroom request, while a quiet hand signal can prompt students to lower their voices.

2. Practice and Reinforce

Use the cues consistently and give students opportunities to practice. Reinforce understanding by acknowledging correct responses with a nod, smile, or thumbs-up.

3. Keep It Consistent and Respectful

Use the same signals regularly so students learn to recognize and respond automatically. Avoid signals that could embarrass or single out students.

Example: During an independent reading block, a student silently raises one finger to request a bathroom break. You make eye contact, nod, and the student quietly leaves without interrupting the class.

When to Use It:

- During independent work, group activities, transitions, or whole-class instruction
- Anytime you want to redirect behavior, give permission, or guide students
- For students who respond well to visual support

Why It Works:

✓ Preserves the classroom tone and momentum

✓ Supports students who struggle with verbal processing

✓ Builds an efficient and respectful learning environment

Attention Signals

Purpose:

To quickly regain student focus in a consistent way.

Description:

This strategy involves using consistent, recognizable auditory or visual cues to get the entire class's attention. These signals help establish classroom rhythm and keep learning time efficient.

How to Use It:

1. **Choose a Signal That Fits You**

   Pick something easy to use in various settings.

2. **Teach the Signal**

   Introduce a clear signal such as:

   - Call and response (e.g., "1-2-3, eyes on me!" / "1-2, eyes on you!")
   - Clapping a pattern for students to echo
   - Ringing a bell or chime
   - Raising a hand silently for students to mirror

3. **Practice and Reinforce**

   Practice the signal regularly at the start of the year or when introducing it for the first time. Model the expected response so students know exactly how to react.

4. **Keep It Consistent and Positive**

   Use the signal consistently and sparingly to preserve its power. When students respond quickly, acknowledge it positively to reinforce the habit.

5. **Reset as Needed**

   If students don't respond right away, wait calmly and repeat the signal until the group follows through without additional reminders.

Example: After a collaborative science project, the room is buzzing with conversation. You say, "If you can hear my voice, clap once!" A few students clap. You repeat, "If you can hear my voice, clap twice!" More students join in. By the third repetition, the whole class is focused and ready for instructions.

When to Use It:

- At the start of a new task or lesson
- When redirecting collective focus
- In noisy or high-energy moments

Why It Works:

- ✓ Creates a reliable system for gaining attention
- ✓ Avoids shouting or repeated reminders
- ✓ Builds shared expectations and rhythm

Name-Dropping

Purpose:

To re-engage or redirect a student without calling them out.

Description:

This strategy involves casually and positively weaving a student's name into your instruction to reinforce connection and bring a student back into the learning moment.

How to Use It:

1. **Incorporate Names Naturally**

   Mention the student's name as part of an example, reflection, or question.

2. **Keep the Tone Positive**

   Use a warm, friendly tone and avoid sounding corrective or sarcastic. Focus on inclusion, not correction.

3. **Make It Meaningful**

   Connect the name drop to something meaningful—such as prior contributions, interests, or relevant content when possible.

4. **Use Flexibly**

   Apply name-dropping proactively to maintain focus before a student gets off track or reactively to bring a student back on task without disruption.

Example: During a science lesson on energy, a student becomes distracted and starts looking around the room. You continue teaching and say, "This part actually reminds me of what Jason said yesterday about energy transfer in roller coasters." Jason refocuses, and the lesson continues smoothly.

When to Use It:

- During whole-group instruction
- While leading discussions or collaborative work
- Anytime gentle redirection is needed without interrupting the flow

Why It Works:

✓ Reconnects students discreetly and respectfully

✓ Maintains momentum and lesson flow

✓ Strengthens student-teacher rapport

Positive Narration

Purpose:

To reinforce expectations by spotlighting desired behavior in real time.

Description:

This strategy involves verbally acknowledging students who are meeting expectations, in the moment, to quietly redirect the class toward on-task behavior. Positive narration reinforces expectations, creates a supportive classroom tone, and shifts attention toward what's going well rather than focusing on misbehavior.

How to Use It:

1. Describe Specific Behaviors

Comment aloud on the positive actions you observe, using students' names when appropriate. Be specific, such as:

- "I see Maria is reading quietly."
- "Nadar has his materials ready and is focused on the task."
- "Kyler's desk is clear and ready for lunch."

2. Reinforce Consistency

Continue to acknowledge students who maintain positive behaviors over time, not just those who are first to follow directions. This helps build habits, not just momentary compliance.

3. Keep It Positive

Focus only on desired behaviors. Avoid using narration to indirectly highlight who is *not* meeting expectations.

4. Use a Calm, Neutral Tone

Deliver narration as part of the classroom routine—not as praise that feels performative or insincere. The goal is to build a culture of positive habits.

Example: During independent writing, you say, "Jamal and Emma are focused and using their checklists to guide their work. That's a great way to make sure everything is included." Other students tune in and begin to mirror the behaviors being acknowledged without you needing to redirect off-task behavior directly.

When to Use It:

- During transitions, independent work, group work, or quiet activities
- Anytime classroom energy needs a reset without confrontation
- As part of daily routines to establish classroom tone

Why It Works:

✓ Reinforces expectations clearly and positively

✓ Encourages self-regulation and peer modeling

✓ Builds trust and emotional safety through acknowledgement

✓ Shifts the classroom tone from correction to celebration

Wait-and-Redirect

Purpose:

To gently refocus attention without escalating behavior.

Description:

This strategy involves using a brief pause paired with calm body language and a neutral prompt to address off-task behavior. It helps maintain lesson flow, reinforces expectations, and preserves student dignity.

How to Use It:

1. Pause the Lesson

Stop speaking or presenting briefly when you notice off-task behavior. Use silence strategically to signal that attention is needed.

2. Use Calm Presence

Make steady, nonverbal eye contact with the student or group.

3. Redirect Respectfully

Use a neutral, encouraging statement to guide students back on track. Keep your tone calm and avoid shaming language.

4. Resume the Lesson Smoothly

Resume teaching without drawing further attention to the behavior. The goal is to regain focus quickly and respectfully.

Example: During a class discussion, a small group begins whispering. You pause mid-sentence, make eye contact with the group, and say, "Let's make sure everyone hears these great ideas." The class refocuses, and you continue without breaking the flow of learning.

When to Use It:

- During instruction, discussions, or group work
- When minor off-task behaviors begin to affect focus

Why It Works:

- ✓ Encourages self-correction without confrontation
- ✓ Maintains a positive, respectful tone
- ✓ Keeps the lesson moving with minimal disruption

Noise Level Chart

Purpose:

To promote self-regulation and focus by setting and reinforcing expectations for classroom volume.

Description:

This strategy involves a visual tool that communicates the appropriate sound level for different classroom activities. It empowers students to monitor their own volume and helps maintain a calm, productive environment.

How to Use It:

1. Create a Simple, Visual Chart

Use numbers, colors, or icons to represent noise levels. For example:

Level 0: Silent (for tests, independent reading, reflection time)

Level 1: Whisper (for partner work or transitions)

Level 2: Group Talk (for collaborative activities)

Level 3: Presentation Voice (for speaking to the whole class)

2. Set Expectations Before Each Task

Before beginning, indicate the expected noise level and give a brief reminder: "We're working at Level 1 for this task."

3. Refer to the Chart Often

Use gentle reminders by directing attention to the chart: "Let's remember we're at Level 1 right now." This promotes self-regulation without constant verbal correction.

4. Acknowledge Success

Recognize when students maintain the correct noise level: "I appreciate how you're all using Level 2 voices during group work—great teamwork."

Example: Before a science experiment, you set the chart to Level 2 and say, "For this part of the activity, we're using group voices to share ideas—but not so loud that other groups can't think." Students check the chart throughout the day to stay on track.

When to Use It:

- During any task where voice volume matters
- To establish and reinforce consistent classroom norms

Why It Works:

✓ Promotes self-awareness and accountability

✓ Reduces the need for repeated verbal reminders

✓ Creates a respectful and focused learning space

Structured Choice

Purpose:

To boost engagement and reduce resistance or noncompliance.

Description:

This strategy involves providing students with structured options for getting to the end goal by increasing ownership and promoting positive behavior.

How to Use It:

1. **Offer Meaningful Options**

   Present two or more options that align with learning goals—such as work location, materials, order of completion, or format of response.

2. **Set Clear Boundaries**

   Frame choices within firm expectations. For example, "You can choose where to work, as long as you stay focused and complete your assignment."

3. **Use Proactively to Prevent Power Struggles**

   Offer choices before behavior escalates. Use choice to defuse tension or re-engage a reluctant student.

4. **Celebrate Positive Choices**

   Reinforce positive choices with simple praise: "Great decision to start with question 2." This reinforces future good choices.

Example: During independent reading time, you give a reluctant student the option to read at their desk, on the carpet, or with a partner. This simple option increases engagement and reduces off-task behavior because the student feels empowered.

When to Use It:

- To reduce conflict or noncompliance
- When a student needs a sense of control
- When there is more than one way to get the same result

Why It Works:

- ✓ Builds autonomy and investment
- ✓ Reduces resistance and defiance
- ✓ Encourages responsible decision-making

Front-Loading Expectations

Purpose:

To proactively set students up for success and prevent misbehaviors.

Description:

This strategy involves reviewing behavior goals before an activity or transition begins so that students are ready to meet expectations.

How to Use It:

1. **State Expectations Clearly**

   Before starting, briefly review what successful behavior looks like. Use specific language, such as, "Remember, during learning stations, we use inside voices and stay with our groups."

2. **Model or Rehearse**

   When appropriate, quickly model the desired behavior or have students practice it before beginning.

3. **Address Predictable Challenges**

   Think ahead to common issues (e.g., lining up, sharing materials) and coach students through solutions before the problem arises.

4. **Use Positive Framing**

   Focus on what you want to see, not what you don't. For example, say, "Show me how you walk safely to the carpet," instead of "Don't run."

Example: Before sending students to work in math centers, you say, "Let's remind ourselves how math stations run. What will our voices sound like? What should we do if we get stuck?" Students respond, reinforcing expectations, setting a positive tone, and reducing the chance of off-task behavior.

When to Use It:

- Before transitions, group work, or independent tasks
- Anytime students would benefit from a reminder of routines
- When there becomes a pattern in common issues

Why It Works:

- ✓ Prevents misbehavior by setting expectations early
- ✓ Builds shared understanding and classroom culture
- ✓ Reduces the need for mid-task redirection

Transition Timers

Purpose:

To maintain momentum and structure during transitions and help students make shifts smoothly.

Description:

This strategy involves using visual or auditory timers to signal when it's time to shift activities. This creates a sense of urgency, keeps transitions efficient, and reduces downtime and disruption.

How to Use It:

1. Give a Verbal Warning

Signal the upcoming transition before starting the timer:

- "You have two minutes before we put away the materials."
- "Finish your sentence—we're wrapping up in thirty seconds."

2. Start the Timer Visibly or Audibly

Use a classroom timer, countdown clock, or chime so students can see or hear the time passing. Visual timers support executive function and time awareness.

3. Narrate the Countdown

Offer reminders as the timer runs:

- "One minute left. Check that your materials are ready."
- "Ten seconds to go. Start wrapping up."

4. Celebrate Smooth Transitions

Acknowledge when students meet the goal:

- "That was our fastest clean-up yet. Nice teamwork."
- "We're ready ahead of time. Love the focus!"

Example: After a group science activity, you set a 60-second timer on the screen and say, "You've got one minute to put away your materials and meet me on the carpet." Students glance at the timer, speed up their tidying, and settle quickly—without multiple reminders or raised voices.

When to Use It:

- During clean-up or setup between subjects
- When rotating through centers or stations
- Before or after recess
- Anytime you want to increase focus and reduce downtime

Why It Works:

✓ Creates structure and predictability

✓ Builds time awareness and self-management

✓ Keeps learning on track with minimal disruption

✓ Reduces nagging and power struggles during transitions

Movement Breaks

Purpose:

To refresh focus and regulate energy by incorporating brief physical activity into the school day.

Description:

This strategy involves offering short, structured opportunities for students to get up, stretch, and move with intention to help them reset their focus, release excess energy, and return to learning refreshed.

How to Use It:

1. Plan Brief Breaks

Schedule 2–5-minute movement breaks during long periods of sitting, test-taking, or focused academic work. Use them proactively—not just after problems arise.

2. Choose Age-Appropriate Activities

Select activities that match the needs of your class and work in your space. Options might include:

- Chair stretches or yoga
- "Simon Says" or freeze dance
- Breathing exercises with movement
- Dance videos

3. Set Clear Expectations

Model how to begin and end a break smoothly. Emphasize participation, not perfection.

4. Signal a Smooth Transition Back to Learning

Use a consistent signal (like a chime, countdown, or callback) to help students refocus and return to task calmly.

Example: After finishing a math test, you play an upbeat, age-appropriate song. Students stand up and follow simple dance moves or free dance to release tension and energy.

When to Use It:

- During long periods of sitting
- After tests or other assessments
- When students appear distracted, tired, or restless
- To proactively build stamina and classroom focus

Why It Works:

✓ Supports self-regulation and stress relief
✓ Increases engagement and attention
✓ Creates a positive and responsive learning environment

Final Thoughts

Classroom management moves are the foundation of a productive learning environment. Great teachers don't just "have control"—they create a space where students want to be on task, where learning feels calm and predictable, and where everyone, including you, can breathe.

Remember, there is no one-size-fits-all approach. By trying different strategies, staying adaptable, and focusing on relationships, you build a toolbox that supports academic growth and social-emotional development.

Ultimately, classroom management is about more than control—it's about connection, respect, and setting students up for success.

Up Next

With your classroom routines and expectations in place, it's time to bring the learning to life. In the next chapter, we'll look at Instructional Moves—strategies that help you teach with clarity, confidence, and purpose.

PUTTING IT INTO PRACTICE

Now that you've seen the why and how behind effective classroom management moves, let's explore what they might look like in real life.

The following scenarios are pulled from common classroom moments—ones that every teacher has faced in some form. Each one invites you to pause, reflect, and consider:

What moves would I make in this moment?

This is where theory meets practice—and where your instincts and toolkit come together.

SCENARIOS

The Side Conversation Spiral

Hallway Tension

Math Group Mayhem

Scenario 1: The Side Conversation Spiral

It's mid-afternoon in your grade 5 class, and you're in the middle of a lesson on the levels of government. You're explaining the purpose of the different levels using a diagram and asking students to take notes as you go.

But the attention in the room is slipping fast.

- Aisha and Sienna are whispering and giggling behind open notebooks.
- River is tapping his pencil on the desk and turning around to talk to Jalen.
- Kenji is tossing an eraser in the air while Mateo tries to ignore him and take notes.
- Several students are clearly distracted, with eyes darting toward the noise instead of the board.

You give a quick redirect— "Eyes up here."

It works for a few seconds... until the side conversations start again.

You try moving closer to the talkers while you teach.

You pause. Wait for silence. It works—briefly.

Then the whispering picks back up.

You feel your energy rising. The lesson is important, but it's being drowned out by side chatter and off-task behavior. You're starting to lose not just their focus but also your own calm.

How Might You Respond?

- What classroom management moves can help you regain attention without turning the lesson into a lecture on behavior?
- How can you reset expectations in a way that's firm, respectful, and effective?
- What proactive routines or strategies might reduce disruptions in the future?

Scenario 2: Hallway Tension

It's just before lunch, and you're heading down the hallway to drop off some papers. As you turn the corner near the lockers, you spot a group of four grade 8 boys loudly goofing around.

One student jumps onto another's back in a piggyback-style wrestling move. Another shouts, "Tackle him!" as a third pushes his friend into a locker—not hard enough to injure, but loud enough to echo down the hall.

Other students nearby stop and stare. One girl quickly turns and walks the other way. The group bursts into laughter.

You're the only adult in sight.

They haven't noticed you yet. You have a split second to decide what to do.

You think:

- Are they just playing?
- Is this about to escalate?
- Should I step in firmly or casually?
- Will they even take me seriously?

You steady your voice and begin to walk toward them.

How Might You Respond?

- How would you approach the group in a way that de-escalates, redirects, and maintains your authority?
- What teacher moves could help you respond without making the situation worse—or ignoring it altogether?
- How would you handle it if one of the students responds with sarcasm or challenges your authority?

Scenario 3: Math Group Mayhem

It's just after recess, your grade 2 class is buzzing with energy. Today's math lesson is all about practicing addition and subtraction strategies using simple word problems. You've set up group stations with task cards, number lines, manipulatives, and dry-erase boards. Each group is expected to read a problem together, talk it through, and solve it as a team.

You've modeled how it works, reviewed the expectations, and assigned roles within each group.

But the moment you say "Go," the room begins to unravel.

In one group, two students are arguing over who gets to use the whiteboard. Another group is loudly singing the "Doubles Rap" instead of solving anything. A third group is more focused on building towers with the cubes than answering questions.

You walk around and notice:

- One student has wandered off to look out the window.
- Another is loudly calling out answers—whether they're needed or not.
- A few students are genuinely trying to solve the problems, but they can't get a word in over the noise.
- Several task cards are untouched.

You give a firm reminder to the class.

The volume dips briefly and some students attempt to refocus...then the noise climbs back up again. You glance at the clock, wondering if anything meaningful is happening at all.

How Might You Respond?

- How might you reset without turning the activity into independent seatwork?
- What classroom management moves could help students stay focused and collaborative?
- What could you change next time to better support self-regulation during math centers?

Chapter 3

Instructional Moves

"She explains things in more than one way. It's like she wants everyone to get it, not just the smart kids." —**Grade 7 student**

A well-run classroom is essential—but it's what you *do* with that time that truly impacts learning. Instructional moves are the heart of teaching. They're how we explain, model, guide, question, and adapt so students can make sense of new concepts and develop deeper understanding.

You don't need to be flashy. You just need to make purposeful moves that keep learning active and accessible.

When students aren't getting it, change the move—not the goal.

Why These Moves Matter

Teaching isn't about delivering content. It's about helping students *make meaning* from it. When your teaching is intentional, students feel it—and learning sticks.

When used well, instructional moves help students:

- Develop understanding, not just memorize facts.
- Engage, no matter their starting point.
- Think critically and independently.
- See you adjust as their needs change.

So, What Are Instructional Moves?

Instructional moves are the intentional choices you make—during planning and in the moment—to guide student learning. Some are structured, like chunking a lesson or creating a visual anchor. Others happen on the fly, like rephrasing a question or modeling your own thinking aloud.

You won't use every move in every lesson. But the more tools you have, the more confident you'll become.

Instructional moves are how we turn good planning into great learning experiences.

Learning From Students

There's a rite of passage nearly every teacher experiences early in their career. It usually goes something like this:

You've planned a fantastic lesson—maybe it's a hands-on math activity with base ten blocks, a creative art project with paint and brushes, or a basketball drills session in the gym. You've planned your lesson, prepped your materials, and in your excitement... you set everything out in advance.

The students walk in and their eyes light up. You feel the energy build—this is going to be great!

Then you begin to talk. Or at least, you try to.

Within seconds, you realize your mistake. No one is listening. They're stacking the cubes, testing the paint colors, or dribbling basketballs before you've even finished your first sentence.

You've lost them before you even began.

It's a classic rookie move—and a powerful reminder that ***timing matters.*** Instructional moves aren't just about what you teach, but when and how you deliver it. In this case, holding off on materials until students understand the task is the move that can make all the difference.

And I promise, every seasoned teacher has done this at least once.

What Makes These Moves Work?

Strong instructional moves make learning clear, meaningful, and doable. They break things down, invite participation, and push students to grow.

Here's what strong instructional moves do:

Guide Learning

You're not just handing out tasks—you're helping students understand *how* to approach them. Modeling, visuals, and step-by-step support show students how to think, not just what to do.

Promote Engagement

Learning happens best when students are actively involved. Cold calling, interactive discussions, or a simple turn-and-talk can bring focus and energy into your lesson.

Support Differentiation

Every class is filled with diverse learners. Moves like scaffolding, sentence starters, and tiered tasks help every student find their way into the learning.

Encourage Critical Thinking

Open-ended prompts and real-world problems ask students to connect ideas and explore deeper meaning—not just recall information.

Foster Autonomy

The goal is for students to take ownership of their learning. Anchor charts, metacognition prompts, and peer teaching build confidence and independence.

In addition, the most effective instructional moves are:

- **Intentional** – You know the why behind what you're doing.
- **Responsive** – You adjust based on what your students need in the moment.
- **Clear** – You break it down, model it, and check for understanding.
- **Inclusive** – You offer multiple ways to access and succeed with the content.

When these qualities are in place, your instruction becomes a launchpad for deeper learning.

Effective instruction meets students where they are —then gently nudges them forward.

Real Talk: What This Looks Like in Action

You're teaching about ecosystems. You introduce the vocabulary. Then you notice blank stares and frantic note copying.
What do you do?

- You model how to create a concept map—***modeling move.***
- You ask, "Why do you think predators and prey need each other to survive?"—***questioning move.***
- You pause for a quick think-pair-share—***processing move.***
- You circulate and check for understanding—***feedback move.***

It takes five minutes. But it shifts the energy. Students are involved, thinking, and making meaning. That's what strong instructional moves do.

You Don't Have to Do It All at Once

Great teaching isn't about using every strategy. It's about choosing a strategy with intention.

Start with a few moves that feel doable:

- Model your thinking when introducing a new concept.
- Ask open-ended questions like, "How do you know?"
- Build an anchor chart together.
- Add a partner task to one lesson each day.

Small shifts can lead to big understanding.

Let's Explore: 15 Instructional Moves

On the following pages, we'll explore fifteen instructional moves that make learning clear, encourage deep thinking, and support all learners:

Activating Prior Knowledge
Questioning
Wait Time
Think-Pair-Share
Modeling

Scaffolding
Chunking
Spiraling
Checking for Understanding
Error Analysis
Anchor Charts
Visuals
Multisensory Approach
Multiple Modalities
Metacognition

Let's take a closer look at each.

Activating Prior Knowledge

Purpose:

To bridge new content with what students already know to spark curiosity, deepen understanding, and boost engagement from the start.

Description:

This strategy involves tapping into students' existing experiences, knowledge, and background before introducing new learning. By making connections up front, students are better able to understand, retain, and engage with unfamiliar material. It also gives insight into misconceptions and knowledge gaps that may need addressing.

How to Use It:

1. Start with a Hook

Begin the lesson with a prompt that taps into students' experiences:

- "Have you ever tried to convince someone of something?"
- "What do you already know about how animals survive in the wild?"

2. Use Active Strategies

Choose a format that gets students thinking and talking:

- Brainstorming
- Quick writes or journal entries
- KWL charts (Know, Want to Know, Learned)
- Turn-and-talk
- Visual prompts or mind maps

3. Make Explicit Connections

Draw clear lines between what students already know and what they are about to learn:

- "Your stories about convincing someone are exactly what persuasive writers do."

- "The migration you saw on a nature show is a survival strategy—we'll dive into more of those today."

4. **Validate Contributions**

   Acknowledge what students bring to the table:

   - "Great connection—yes, that's a real-life example of cause and effect."
   - "That background knowledge is going to help you a lot in this unit."

Example: Before launching a lesson on persuasive writing, you ask, "Have you ever tried to get someone to see things your way—like which game to play or whether to stay up late?" Students share experiences, and you link their real-world persuasion strategies to upcoming writing techniques such as giving reasons, providing examples, and making emotional appeals.

When to Use It:

- At the start of a new unit or lesson
- When introducing complex or abstract concepts
- Before review sessions to gauge readiness
- When students seem disconnected or unsure of relevance

Why It Works:

✓ Builds on existing knowledge for better retention

✓ Increases student engagement from the start

✓ Surfaces misconceptions that can be addressed early

✓ Affirms student voices and builds confidence

Questioning

Purpose:

To promote deeper thinking, assess understanding, and foster curiosity through intentional and varied questions.

Description:

This strategy involves using open-ended and higher-order questions to engage students in meaningful dialogue. It supports active participation, stimulates critical thinking, and helps check for understanding throughout the learning process.

How to Use It:

1. Plan a Variety of Question Types

Include a mix of question types to encourage students to explain, analyze, evaluate, or reflect:

- "What evidence supports your answer?"
- "How are these two ideas connected?"
- "What would happen if...?"

2. Engage All Students

Pose questions to the whole class, small groups, or individual students.

3. Allow Wait Time

Pause after asking to let students think before answering. This encourages quality responses and reduces pressure.

4. Use Follow-Up Prompts

Prompt students to expand or go deeper:

- "Can you tell me more?"
- "What makes you think that?"
- "Does anyone see it differently?"

5. Encourage Risk-Taking

Normalize mistakes and multiple perspectives:

- "Interesting take—there's more than one way to see this."
- "Thanks for sharing that, even if you weren't sure."

Example: During a novel discussion, you ask, "Why do you think the author chose this setting?" After a student responds, you follow up with, "Imagine the story took place somewhere else—how might that change the tone or plot?" Students begin to consider how time and place shape the narrative, deepening their analysis.

When to Use It:

- During direct instruction or mini lessons
- While guiding discussions or book talks
- As part of group tasks or problem-solving
- Anytime you want to check understanding or spark reflection

Why It Works:

✓ Sparks curiosity and creativity
✓ Promotes active listening and discussion
✓ Encourages all students to participate
✓ Builds critical thinking and metacognition

Wait Time

Purpose:

To give students space to think deeply, process ideas, and craft more thoughtful responses.

Description:

This strategy involves intentionally pausing after asking a question or hearing a student's response. These moments of silence may feel small but have a big impact. They communicate that thinking is valued more than speed and that every student deserves a chance to process and contribute.

How to Use It:

1. Pause After Asking a Question

Ask your question, then wait—silently—for about 10–15 seconds:

- "Why do you think the character made that choice?" (*pause and look around*)

2. Pause After a Response

Give space after a student answers. This invites additions, clarifications, or deeper follow-up.

3. Use Nonverbal Cues

Maintain eye contact, nod, and use open body language to show you're holding space—not ending the moment. Resist the urge to jump in too soon.

4. Prompt for Deeper Thinking

Use gentle prompts to stretch student thinking:

- "What makes you say that?"
- "Can anyone build on that idea?"
- "How does that connect to what we learned yesterday?"

5. Normalize Silence

Let students know that taking time to think is a strength:

- "It's okay to pause before answering. That's how we grow our thinking."

Example: During a grade 3 math lesson, you ask, "Why do you think the answer is twenty-four?" Instead of calling on the first raised hand, you wait silently for ten seconds. A student responds, and you pause again before asking, "Can you walk us through how you solved it?" This leads to a rich discussion of multiple multiplication strategies.

When to Use It:

- After posing open-ended questions
- During class discussions
- When students seem hesitant or unsure
- While teaching complex or new content

Why It Works:

✓ Increases the quality and depth of responses
✓ Encourages broader participation
✓ Builds student confidence and reflection skills
✓ Shifts the focus from speed to thoughtful thinking

Think-Pair-Share

Purpose:

To boost participation and deepen understanding by giving every student time to think, talk, and share ideas.

Description:

This strategy is a cooperative learning approach that gives all students the chance to process ideas individually, discuss their thinking with a partner, and share responses with the whole class. It promotes deeper thinking, active listening, and increased participation, especially for students who may be hesitant to speak up in large groups.

How to Use It:

1. Pose a Thoughtful Question or Prompt

Ask an open-ended question that invites explanation, connection, or analysis:

- "What do you think the author's message is?"
- "How might this idea apply in real life?"

2. Think

Give students silent time to jot down their ideas. This ensures everyone has time to process before sharing.

3. Pair

Have students turn to a partner to share their thoughts. Set a clear time limit for each partner to speak and encourage equal participation.

- "You each have one minute to explain your thinking."

4. Share

Invite pairs to share their ideas with the whole class. This can be done by calling on random pairs, asking for volunteers, or collecting ideas on a chart or whiteboard.

5. **Debrief**

   Summarize key takeaways and connect the discussion back to your learning goal:

   - "Let's review some of the themes we uncovered together."

Example: During a reading lesson, you ask, "What lesson do you think the character learned?" Students jot down ideas, discuss with a partner, and three pairs share with the class. You highlight contrasting interpretations to foster rich discussion.

When to Use It:

- To kick off a discussion or explore a new topic
- To check for understanding in the middle of a lesson
- After reading, watching, or exploring something new
- Anytime you want to increase participation and peer interaction

Why It Works:

✓ Encourages every student to think before responding

✓ Builds confidence and communication skills

✓ Supports language development and listening skills

✓ Promotes inclusive classroom dialogue

Modeling

Purpose:

To demonstrate a skill, strategy, or behavior to set clear expectations and guide students toward success.

Description:

This strategy involves showing students exactly what a task looks like when done well. It allows learners to see the thinking, choices, and actions involved before trying it themselves. It supports visual learning, reduces confusion, and builds student confidence—especially with unfamiliar content or multi-step processes.

How to Use It:

1. Set Clear Expectations

Before modeling, explain the task and tell students exactly what to watch for. Use phrases such as:

- "Watch how I..."
- "Notice what I do when..."

2. Think Aloud

As you model, verbalize your thought process step by step. This helps students understand not just *what* to do but *how* and *why* decisions are made.

- "I'm starting with the topic sentence, so the reader knows my main idea."
- "I'm double-checking my answer to make sure it makes sense."

3. Gradually Release Responsibility

After modeling, have students try the task with guided support before expecting independent practice. Use a "we do" step.

- "Let's try the first part together."
- "Now, you try the next step while I help."

Example: During an art lesson, you demonstrate how to blend watercolor paints and say, "First, I'll wet my brush and add a small amount of blue. Now watch as I rinse my brush slightly and add yellow to create a smooth green gradient. Notice how I'm controlling the amount of water to avoid puddles." Students observe, ask questions, and then begin their own blending with support.

When to Use It:

- When introducing new tasks, routines, tools, or skills
- During writing, math, science experiments, the arts, or physical education
- Before partner or independent work
- Anytime you want students to visualize what success looks like

Why It Works:

✓ Makes abstract tasks concrete and accessible

✓ Supports visual and auditory learners

✓ Builds confidence through clear guidance

✓ Prepares students for greater independence and success

Scaffolding

Purpose:

To support students in mastering new skills or concepts by breaking learning into manageable steps and gradually increasing independence.

Description:

This strategy involves providing temporary, targeted support as students learn something new. It helps reduce overwhelm, builds confidence, and ensures success along the way. As students gain skill and understanding, the supports are slowly removed, allowing them to take full ownership of their learning.

How to Use It:

1. Break Tasks into Steps

Divide complex tasks into smaller, more achievable parts. Guide students through one step at a time to prevent overwhelm.

- "Let's start by brainstorming, then we'll move on to drafting."

2. Use Support Tools

Offer scaffolds that help students begin with structure:

- Sentence starters
- Graphic organizers
- Checklists
- Guiding questions

3. Model and Practice Together

Start with teacher-led examples or shared practice—the "I do" and "we do" stages. This builds understanding and reduces anxiety.

- "Watch me do the first one, then we'll try one together."

4. **Gradually Release Responsibility**

   As students gain skill, remove supports and encourage independent practice—the "you do" phase. Adjust the level of help based on student needs.

   - "You're ready to try this on your own. Use the examples as a guide."

5. **Monitor and Adjust**

   Pay attention to how students are progressing. Some may need scaffolds longer, while others are ready for independence sooner.

Example: During a writing lesson, you first model a paragraph ("I do"), then work with students using sentence frames ("We do"), and finally remove supports as students write independently ("You do"). Visuals like anchor charts and checklists remain available for reference.

When to Use It:

- When introducing challenging or unfamiliar concepts
- With students who need extra guidance or confidence
- While teaching multi-step processes
- Anytime you want to promote mastery without frustration

Why It Works:

✓ Builds confidence and competence gradually

✓ Makes complex tasks more accessible

✓ Supports diverse learners at their level

✓ Fosters independence and long-term success

Chunking

Purpose:

To make complex tasks or content more manageable by breaking them into smaller, digestible parts.

Description:

This strategy involves breaking complex information or tasks into smaller, manageable parts to improve understanding, reduce cognitive overload, and support retention. It helps students process new content step by step, building confidence as they master each part.

How to Use It:

1. Identify Key Components

Look at the concept, lesson, or task and break it into logical sections or steps. Focus on one part at a time.

- "Today, let's focus first on brainstorming our arguments against non-renewable energy."

2. Teach in Small Segments

Present each chunk separately. Check for understanding before moving on to the next piece. Use mini lessons, guided practice, or short activities to reinforce each part.

- "Now that we've brainstormed our ideas, let's review how to write an opening paragraph."

3. Use Visual Tools

Help students keep track of steps using:

- Graphic organizers
- Anchor charts
- Step-by-step lists

4. Connect the Chunks

Bring everything together and show how the parts form a whole:

- "Now that we've practiced each part of a 5-paragraph essay, let's begin our rough drafts on non-renewable energy."

Example: During a writing lesson, you break the paragraph-writing process into chunks. First, students learn how to craft a clear topic sentence. Next, they focus on adding supporting details with facts and examples. Then, they practice writing a strong closing sentence. Finally, after each component is modeled and practiced separately, students bring the pieces together to write full paragraphs with confidence.

When to Use It:

- While teaching multi-step skills or processes
- When introducing new or dense content
- With students who benefit from step-by-step instruction
- Anytime a task feels overwhelming or cognitively demanding

Why It Works:

✓ Reduces cognitive overload and frustration

✓ Supports understanding and retention

✓ Builds confidence through small wins

✓ Makes complex tasks feel achievable

Spiraling

Purpose:

To reinforce and deepen understanding of key concepts and skills.

Description:

This strategy involves introducing core ideas early and then revisiting them repeatedly over time in different contexts. It strengthens long-term retention, builds connections between topics, and supports mastery by allowing students to encounter the same concepts in new and more challenging ways.

How to Use It:

1. **Introduce Core Concepts Early**

   Teach the foundational skill or concept at a basic level, making sure students have an initial understanding.

2. **Layer New Learning on Old**

   Connect new lessons to what students have already learned:

   - "Remember when we learned about fractions? Today, we'll use that to understand ratios."

3. **Design Cumulative Practice**

   Mix review items from past units into current lessons or assignments to strengthen recall and application:

   - "Let's start with three warm-up problems from last month's geometry unit."

4. **Use Multiple Exposures**

   Plan opportunities to revisit and extend concepts weeks or months later in different contexts. Think of it as a cycle: *teach—review—apply in new ways.*

Example: During math class, you introduce fractions early in the year. Later, fractions are revisited during units on ratios, decimals, and measurement. Each return adds new complexity while reinforcing earlier skills, helping students retain knowledge and see its relevance in multiple areas.

When to Use It:

- All year long for essential skills in literacy, math, and science
- When you want concepts to be mastered, not just memorized for a test
- In subjects where knowledge builds over time

Why It Works:

- ✓ Improves long-term retention
- ✓ Strengthens connections between topics
- ✓ Prevents "learn it and forget it" cycles
- ✓ Supports mastery through repeated, varied practice

Checking for Understanding

Purpose:

To monitor student learning in real time so you can address misconceptions and adjust instruction before moving on.

Description:

This strategy involves using quick, informal methods during instruction to see how well students grasp new material. It gives teachers instant feedback to guide pacing, reteaching, or enrichment. This ongoing check ensures no student is left behind and prevents small misunderstandings from becoming bigger gaps.

How to Use It:

1. Ask a Targeted Question

Pause during the lesson to pose a question, problem, or prompt directly related to the learning goal.

2. Use Quick Response Methods

Gather student responses using simple, low-stakes techniques such as:

- Thumbs up/thumbs down
- Mini whiteboards
- Quick polls or digital response tools

3. Analyze the Responses

Scan for patterns in student answers. Are most students ready to move on, or do you need to revisit part of the lesson?

4. Respond in the Moment

Use the information to reteach, clarify, slow the pace, or extend the lesson depending on what students need.

Example: During a science lesson on states of matter, you ask, "Is ice melting into water a chemical change? Thumbs up for yes, thumbs down for no." Most students show thumbs down, but a few are unsure. You take a moment to review physical versus chemical changes with real-life examples before continuing.

When to Use It:

- While introducing new content
- During guided practice
- Before moving to independent work
- Anytime you want to confirm learning is on track

Why It Works:

✓ Catches misunderstandings early

✓ Guides instructional decisions in real time

✓ Keeps all students engaged in the learning process

✓ Supports differentiated instruction

Error Analysis

Purpose:

To turn mistakes into powerful learning tools by helping students identify, understand, and correct errors.

Description:

This strategy involves examining mistakes—either in student work or provided samples—to uncover misconceptions, strengthen understanding, and improve problem-solving skills. By shifting the focus from "getting it right" to learning from the process, students build resilience, develop a growth mindset, and deepen content mastery.

How to Use It:

1. Present Errors as Learning Opportunities

Share examples of common mistakes or have students reflect on their own work:

- "Here's a problem with a small place value error—let's find it."

Frame mistakes as natural and valuable to the learning process.

2. Guide Students to Analyze

Ask reflective questions:

- "Where did the thinking go off track?"
- "What could you try differently next time?"

Encourage them to explain the correct process in their own words.

3. Model the Process

Work through an example aloud, showing your thought process as you identify and fix the mistake.

4. Include Peer and Self-Review

Use a combination of self-reflection and partner work to practice locating and correcting errors.

Example: During a math lesson, you present a multiplication problem with a place value error. Students work in pairs to locate the mistake, discuss why it happened, and correct it. This leads to a stronger grasp of multiplication and place value concepts.

When to Use It:

- After quizzes, tests, or practice activities
- During math problem-solving, writing revisions, or science lab reports
- In test prep to strengthen reasoning skills
- Anytime you want students to reflect on and learn from their mistakes

Why It Works:

✓ Clarifies misconceptions early

✓ Encourages a growth mindset

✓ Builds metacognitive and problem-solving skills

✓ Helps students transfer learning to new situations

Anchor Charts

Purpose:

To provide a visual, student-created reference tool that captures key learning and supports independence.

Description:

This strategy involves creating collaborative visual aids that record important concepts, strategies, processes, or reminders from lessons. They act as "learning anchors" that students can revisit to refresh their memory, guide independent work, and strengthen retention.

How to Use It:

1. Create Charts Collaboratively

Build the chart with students during the lesson, capturing their ideas, examples, and strategies in real time:

- "Let's add that great idea to our problem-solving chart."

2. Keep It Clear and Visual

Use short phrases, bullet points, diagrams, and color coding. Focus on essential takeaways rather than too much detail.

3. Display and Refer Back Often

Hang charts where students can see them and use them during lessons, centers, or independent practice.

4. Update and Refresh

Add new information or create revised charts together as understanding deepens. Remove or replace outdated ones to keep the display relevant.

Example: During math, you and your students create a **Problem-Solving** anchor chart with steps such as:

(1) Read the problem carefully.

(2) Circle the important information.

(3) Choose a strategy (draw a picture, make a chart, write an equation).

(4) Solve the problem.

(5) Check your work and explain your thinking.

Students refer back to the chart during math centers and independent tasks to guide their work and build independence.

When to Use It:

- When introducing new concepts, strategies, or classroom routines
- During literacy, math, science, or social-emotional learning lessons
- In mini lessons, small groups, or review sessions to reinforce learning

Why It Works:

✓ Makes learning visible and accessible

✓ Encourages student ownership and self-direction

✓ Provides a consistent reference for review

✓ Supports retention and transfer of skills

Visuals

Purpose:

To clarify concepts, increase engagement, and support retention by pairing content with meaningful visual aids.

Description:

This strategy involves using visuals—such as images, charts, diagrams, and videos—to help students process and organize information, especially when learning abstract or complex ideas. When used intentionally, visuals make content more concrete, accessible, and memorable for all learners.

How to Use It:

1. Choose Relevant Visuals

Select visuals that directly support the lesson goal. Ensure they are accurate, age-appropriate, and easy to interpret.

2. Integrate Visuals Purposefully

Introduce visuals at key points to illustrate processes, break down information, or highlight important details.

3. Encourage Active Interaction

Engage students actively by having them:

- Label diagrams
- Interpret graphs
- Compare images
- Predict what will happen next in a video
- Discuss how the visual connects to the topic

4. Pair with Clear Explanation

Combine visuals with verbal or written explanations to reinforce meaning. This dual coding approach helps ideas stick.

5. **Support All Learners**

   Use visuals to aid multilingual learners, visual learners, and students who benefit from multiple representations of information.

Example: During a science lesson on life cycles, you display a large diagram of a butterfly's four stages: egg, caterpillar, chrysalis, butterfly. As each stage is highlighted, you explains what happens. Students label their own diagrams and discuss how the stages connect. The lesson concludes with a short video of a butterfly emerging, reinforcing the visual learning.

When to Use It:

- When introducing new or complex content
- To illustrate timelines, life cycles, scientific processes, or math procedures
- When summarizing or reviewing key concepts
- Anytime visual representation will make learning clearer and more engaging

Why It Works:

- ✓ Makes abstract concepts concrete
- ✓ Improves comprehension and recall
- ✓ Supports diverse learning needs
- ✓ Increases engagement through multiple modes of learning

Multisensory Approach

Purpose:

To strengthen learning by activating multiple sensory pathways in the brain at the same time—boosting engagement, understanding, and retention.

Description:

This strategy involves combining sight, sound, touch, and movement to help students learn more effectively. By activating different parts of the brain, it makes lessons more interactive, concrete, and memorable. This method benefits all students, but it's especially powerful for learners who need multiple forms of input to stay focused or grasp challenging material.

How to Use It:

1. **Combine Senses in Instruction**

   Pair visuals (charts, diagrams, videos) with auditory elements (read-alouds, discussions, music) and kinesthetic activities (manipulatives, role-play, movement) to reinforce concepts.

2. **Encourage "Say It, See It, Do It"**

   Have students speak answers aloud, write or draw their ideas, and physically interact with materials.

3. **Incorporate Tools and Materials**

   Use tactile items, models, technology, or hands-on experiments to make abstract concepts more concrete.

4. **Adapt for Diverse Learners**

   Adjust activities to meet the needs of multilingual learners, students with learning differences, or those who need more active engagement.

Example: During a phonics lesson, you say a word and students repeat it aloud. They clap out the syllables, trace the letters in sand, and then write the word on whiteboards. This sequence engages sight, sound, and touch, reinforcing the spelling pattern.

When to Use It:

- When introducing new content
- When supporting struggling learners
- When reviewing or reteaching difficult concepts
- When teaching across subjects to enhance comprehension and retention

Why It Works:

✓ Activates multiple brain pathways for stronger memory

✓ Makes abstract ideas more concrete and accessible

✓ Increases engagement and participation

✓ Supports a wide range of learning needs and styles

Multiple Modalities

Purpose:

To reach and engage all learners by teaching through a variety of methods—visual, auditory, kinesthetic, and written.

Description:

This strategy involves presenting content in multiple ways so students can access, process, and demonstrate learning through their strengths. By reinforcing concepts across different formats, it increases engagement, deepens understanding, and makes lessons more inclusive.

How to Use It:

1. Mix Teaching Approaches

Plan lessons that include:

- Visuals: diagrams, videos, charts, anchor charts
- Auditory: storytelling, discussions, music, podcasts
- Kinesthetic: experiments, role-play, building models, hands-on tools
- Written: notetaking, journaling, creative writing, graphic organizers

2. Offer Multiple Ways to Engage

Allow students to interact with the content in different formats:

- Draw a diagram
- Build a model
- Write a summary
- Teach a peer

3. Use Varied Tools

Incorporate manipulatives, multimedia, interactive notebooks, and movement-based learning to deepen understanding.

4. **Assess in Different Formats**

   Provide choices or rotate assessments, such as oral presentations, visual projects, written reports, or demonstrations.

Example: During a science lesson on the water cycle, you:

Show an animated video (Visual)

Use a diagram on the board (Visual)

Lead a hands-on evaporation experiment (Kinesthetic)

Facilitate a group discussion (Auditory)

Have students write a reflection on what they learned (Written)

When to Use It:

- When introducing new material
- For reinforcing complex or abstract concepts
- For reviewing in creative, engaging ways
- When supporting students with different learning styles and needs

Why It Works:

✓ Provides multiple entry points for understanding

✓ Reinforces learning through varied channels

✓ Increases engagement and participation

✓ Helps all learners connect with the content in ways that suit them best

Metacognition

Purpose:

To help students become aware of and take control of their own thinking to improve learning, problem-solving, and self-reflection.

Description:

This strategy involves "thinking about one's own thinking." Metacognition enables students to plan, monitor, and evaluate their learning processes. When learners understand how they learn, they can choose strategies more effectively, adjust when something isn't working, and become more independent and resilient.

How to Use It:

1. **Model Thinking Aloud**

   Share your thought process during a task:

   - "I'm not sure about this answer—let me check it another way."
   - "I think I need to slow down and reread to be sure I understand."

2. **Use Reflection Prompts**

   Ask guiding questions:

   - "What strategy did you use?"
   - "Why did you choose it?"
   - "Did it work? What will you try next time?"

3. **Teach Self-Monitoring**

   Encourage students to pause and check in with themselves:

   - "Do I understand this so far?"
   - "What's my next step?"

4. **Incorporate Learning Journals**

   Have students track strategies, challenges, and adjustments in journals, logs, or exit slips to build ongoing awareness.

Example: During a literacy lesson, you read a paragraph aloud and say, "I'm realizing I didn't fully understand that section, so I'm going to reread it slowly and look for clues." Students then practice the same strategy, noting in their journals when they needed to pause and clarify while reading.

When to Use It:

- During reading comprehension, writing, and problem-solving tasks
- When introducing new strategies that require monitoring and adjustment
- Anytime you want students to become more reflective, strategic, and self-directed learners

Why It Works:

✓ Builds self-awareness and independence

✓ Improves problem-solving and adaptability

✓ Encourages reflection and strategic thinking

✓ Helps students transfer skills across subjects

Final Thoughts

The most effective teachers aren't the ones with the fanciest lessons or the flashiest tech—they're the ones who know how to *move* with intention. They guide learning like a good conversation: thoughtful, responsive, and real.

Instructional moves are how you make learning come alive. They help students *do the work of thinking,* not just listen to someone else's.

Your classroom is a space where minds grow. Every move you make shapes that growth. When you choose to model your thinking, ask just the right question or pause to let a student struggle productively, you're doing more than teaching content. You're helping students become learners—and you're transforming how students see themselves and what they're capable of.

Up Next

In the next chapter, we'll explore a different kind of move—the ones that strengthen connection. Students do their best thinking when they feel known and supported. Relationship-building moves lay that groundwork. When students feel a sense of trust and belonging, they're more open, more engaged, and more willing to take intellectual risks.

Let's look at how those relationships take root and grow—one intentional move at a time.

PUTTING IT INTO PRACTICE

Now that you've seen the why and how behind effective instructional moves, let's explore what they might look like in real life.

The following scenarios are pulled from common classroom moments—ones that every teacher has faced in some form. Each one invites you to pause, reflect, and consider:

What moves would I make in this moment?

This is where theory meets practice—and where your instincts and toolkit come together.

SCENARIOS

Lost in the Lesson

Why Do We Have to Learn This?

When the Steps Don't Stick

Scenario 1: Lost in the Lesson

It's Tuesday afternoon, and your grade 8 class is diving into a new science unit on chemical changes. You've planned a structured, content-rich lesson with visuals, vocabulary, and examples. Your goal is to explain the difference between physical and chemical changes and introduce key concepts like reactivity and evidence of change.

You start strong with a real-life example—baking a cake—and link it to the idea of irreversible change. Then you move into a mini lesson with definitions and notes, supported by a short video and a guided worksheet.

But about ten minutes in, the energy shifts.

Some students are zoned out, staring at the clock or scribbling in notebooks. A couple are whispering to each other and passing notes. A few have their hands up—but only to ask, "Do we have to write all this down?" or "Will this be on the test?"

You notice:

- A few students are still copying your notes word-for-word without understanding them.
- Others are clearly lost but won't ask for help.
- When you pause to ask a check-for-understanding question, only one or two students respond.
- A quiet, capable student finally says, "Wait. What's a chemical change again?"

You suddenly realize you've been talking for almost twenty minutes, and most of the class is no longer with you.

How Might You Respond?

- What instructional moves could you use to re-engage the class and clarify key concepts?
- How could you adjust your pacing or approach in the moment?
- What strategies might support deeper understanding for a diverse group of learners?

Scenario 2: Why Do We Have to Learn This?

It's the start of a new unit on persuasive writing in your grade 7 class. You begin by reviewing the elements of a strong argument—claim, evidence, and reasoning—and ask students to brainstorm issues they care about.

But instead of enthusiasm, you're met with eye rolls and disengagement.

- Omar puts his head down and says, "This is boring."
- Sawyer asks, "Can we just write about whatever? Why does it have to be an argument?"
- Leo doodles across the margins of his organizer, while Tessa raises her hand to ask, "What's the point of this, anyway?"

You pause.

This isn't about confusion—they understand what persuasive writing is. The problem is—they don't care. They're not connecting.

You realize that in this moment, what's needed isn't re-teaching the content. It's shifting your approach to *how* the content is introduced and made meaningful.

How Might You Respond?

- What instructional moves can you use to build relevance, curiosity, and buy-in?
- How can you scaffold the lesson so that students feel empowered to write about real, meaningful topics?
- What strategies might re-engage them without abandoning your objective?

Scenario 3: When the Steps Don't Stick

It's just before lunch in your grade 4 classroom, and you're teaching a math lesson on long division. You've modeled two examples on the board, talking through each step and asking students to copy them into their notebooks.

Then, you give them a few practice problems to try on their own.

You step back and wait for pencils to start moving—but they don't.

- Ben raises his hand and says, "I don't get it at all."
- Leila stares at her page, frozen, quietly whispering the steps to herself but not writing anything down.
- Dmitri skips ahead and writes the final answer without showing his work.
- Mei, who normally finishes first, turns to her neighbor and says, "I'm confused. Did we do this before?"

You scan the room and notice that several students are either stuck, off-task, or copying from a friend. The confidence just isn't there.

You realize that although you explained it clearly from your perspective, they didn't *see* it. They didn't *grasp* it. And now the lesson is stalling.

How Might You Respond?

- What instructional moves can you use to re-teach or break the concept down in a different way?
- How might you check for understanding without singling students out or wasting time?
- What scaffolds or tools could help bridge the gap between modeling and independence?

Chapter 4

Relationship-Building Moves

"He listens, like what we say really matters." —**Grade 5 student**

Let's be honest, students don't just show up ready to learn because you have a great lesson plan. They show up *for you*. When students feel seen, valued, and supported, everything else works better. The classroom feels calmer. The energy shifts. The learning clicks.

Relationship-building isn't a "nice extra." It's foundational. You don't need to be their best friend or know the latest TikTok trends. You just need to show up consistently, with care and curiosity.

That's where relationship-building moves come in. These are the small, intentional choices you make every day that tell students: *You matter here.*

Why These Moves Matter

Strong teacher-student relationships don't just make the classroom feel better—they make it work better. When students trust their teacher, they take more risks, try harder, and bounce back more easily.

Relationship-building moves help you:

- Create a classroom where students feel emotionally and physically safe.
- Increase engagement through connection and belonging.
- Reduce misbehavior by building mutual trust.
- Support social-emotional growth.
- Boost academic performance.
- Respond more effectively to student needs.

So, What Are Relationship-Building Moves?

Relationship-building moves are the everyday practices that build trust, connection, and community. Some are planned, like greeting students at the door. Others happen in the moment, like noticing when something feels off or celebrating a small win.

They don't require extra time or a big personality. They just require a genuine interest in your students as people.

When students know you care, they care more too—about their work, their behavior, and each other.

Be human first. Teacher second.

The Moment of Choice

Lunch supervision in the intermediate hallway is never boring. On any given day, you might encounter tears, drama, loud noises, objects flying, or students wandering into the wrong classroom.

To survive it, especially if you're not one of their regular teachers, you need strong teacher moves. The kind that goes beyond rules and routines.

For me, I lean on **relationship-building moves** in these moments. The more I know about the students—their interests, friend groups, personalities—the more likely I am to get their cooperation when needed.

One afternoon, I noticed a grade 8 student repeatedly bouncing a basketball and launching it against the wall. The hallway was crowded and starting to get noisy. I had a choice to make.

I could walk straight up and demand the ball—use my authority to shut it down. Or I could use what I knew about this student to connect with him.

I had never taught him, but I had made efforts to get to know him during previous supervisions. So, I knew he played on the school basketball team.

I chose connection.

As I approached the group, I asked, "How was your game last night?"

He stopped instantly.

He smiled, lowered the ball, and began telling me. I listened—giving him my full attention. Then I reminded him, gently: "No bouncing the basketball in the hall."

He nodded. "Okay, sorry Miss."

No power struggle. No confiscated ball. And he didn't bounce it again ***that*** day.

That moment wasn't about control—it was about connection. A well-timed relationship move diffused the situation and maintained the dignity of everyone involved. That's what teacher moves are all about.

What Makes These Moves Work?

Relationship-building moves aren't about grand gestures. They're about the small, consistent ways you show students they matter.

These moves help create a classroom where students feel safe, valued, and supported. Not just as learners, but as people. When students feel like they belong, they show up more fully, engage more deeply, and learn more effectively.

Here's what strong relationship-building moves do:

Create a Nurturing Environment

Students are more likely to thrive when they feel known and cared for. Simple things like learning their names quickly, celebrating birthdays, or noticing when something's off, help create a sense of belonging.

Increase Engagement and Motivation

When students feel like you see them, they're more likely to invest effort. A note of encouragement, a quick chat about their weekend, or simply asking how they're doing can go a long way in building that bridge.

Reduce Behavioral Issues

Many misbehaviors are rooted in disconnection. When students trust you and feel respected, they're more likely to regulate their behavior and work through challenges collaboratively.

Foster Social-Emotional Growth

Relationship-building isn't just about rapport. It's about modeling and teaching emotional intelligence. Moves like resolving conflicts calmly, checking in regularly, and showing empathy help students build important life skills.

Support Academic Success

Students tend to work harder for teachers who believe in them—and who they believe care about them. When students feel supported, they're more willing to take risks, make mistakes, and keep going when things get hard.

In addition, the most effective relationship-building strategies are:

- **Genuine** – Students know when you're being real. Be yourself.
- **Consistent** – Trust builds over time. Keep showing up.
- **Inclusive** – Go beyond the easy-to-like students.
- **Responsive** – Notice what's happening beneath the surface.
- **Patient** – Some students take time. Stay steady.

When these qualities are in place, your classroom becomes a place where students feel safe enough to show up as their full selves. And that's when the real learning happens.

**Every student wants to feel seen.
Especially the ones who pretend not to.**

Real Talk: What This Looks Like in Action

It's Thursday morning. One student comes in with their head down. Another is bouncing off the walls. Others look half asleep.

What do you do?

- Greet each student by name—***connection move.***
- Quietly check in with the one having a rough morning—***empathy move.***
- Give the high-energy student a movement-based "job" —***responsiveness move.***
- Start class with a light check-in: "What's something you're looking forward to today?"—***community-building move.***

These moments take minutes. But they shape the tone of the day.

You Don't Have to Do It All at Once

You don't need to build a deep connection with every student immediately. Start with what feels natural:

- Greet students at the door with eye contact and a smile.
- Invite a "what's working" classroom discussion.
- Make space for one personal conversation with a student each day.
- Notice and shout out kind or helpful actions.

Then, keep going. Keep noticing. Keep showing up. Relationship-building isn't a strategy—it's a mindset.

Let's Explore: 13 Relationship-Building Moves

On the following pages, we'll explore thirteen relationship-building moves you can use to build connection, boost motivation, and create a classroom culture where all students feel like they belong:

Greeting at the Door
Using Student Names
Incorporating Student Interests
Sharing About Yourself
Active Listening
Using Humor
Positive Reinforcement
"What's Working" Conversations
Highlighting Strengths
Celebrating Successes
Two-by-Ten Strategy
Restorative Circles
Community Circles

Let's take a closer look at each.

Greeting at the Door

Purpose:

To set a positive tone, build relationships, and create a sense of belonging from the moment students enter the classroom.

Description:

This strategy involves standing at the classroom door and greeting students to establish connection and emotional safety before learning begins. A simple, intentional greeting helps students feel seen, valued, and ready to learn. This daily ritual helps foster community and reduce behavior issues.

How to Use It:

1. Be Present at the Door

Stand at the classroom entrance as students arrive. Make eye contact, smile warmly, and welcome each student individually.

2. Use Names and Personalization

Greet students by name to strengthen rapport. Offer options like a handshake, high-five, fist bump, or wave—letting students choose what feels comfortable.

3. Check in Emotionally

Use this moment to gauge how students are feeling. Notice their body language, mood, or energy level. If a student seems upset or withdrawn, make a mental note to check in later.

4. Build Consistency

Make greetings part of your daily routine. A predictable, positive start builds trust and reinforces classroom community over time.

Example: At the start of the day, you stand at the door and greet each student by name. When Cindy arrives, you say, "Good morning, Cindy! How was your soccer game yesterday?" Cindy smiles, gives a quick update, and takes her seat feeling noticed and valued.

When to Use It:

- Every morning as students arrive
- After recess or lunch
- During class transitions

Why It Works:

✓ Creates a welcoming, inclusive atmosphere

✓ Strengthens student-teacher relationships

✓ Provides quick insight into student emotions

✓ Sets a positive, focused tone for learning

Using Student Names

Purpose:

To build connection, show respect, and foster a sense of belonging by intentionally using students' names in daily interactions.

Description:

This strategy involves prioritizing correct pronunciation and weaving students' names naturally into daily interactions to strengthen relationships and promote equity. Using names may seem simple, but it's one of the most powerful ways to create a culture of respect and inclusion.

How to Use It:

1. **Learn Names Early**

   Make learning every student's name your top priority in the first days of school. Use name tents, games, or seating charts to help.

2. **Prioritize Correct Pronunciation**

   Ask students to teach you how to say their names properly and practice until you get it right. If you're unsure, ask again—this shows respect.

3. **Use Names Purposefully**

   Say students' names when greeting them, asking questions, offering feedback, or narrating positive behavior. Integrate names naturally into lessons to maintain attention and connection.

4. **Balance Attention**

   Make a point to use all students' names regularly, not just those who speak up often or need redirection. This ensures every student feels included and valued.

Example: During a math lesson, you say, "Let's look at Elijah's strategy for solving this problem. He showed us a creative way to break apart the numbers." This highlights Elijah's contribution, reinforces engagement, and models respect for student thinking.

When to Use It:

- During daily greetings and check-ins
- While leading discussions or transitions
- When giving feedback or recognizing effort
- Throughout lessons to maintain attention and connection

Why It Works:

✓ Builds trust and belonging

✓ Reinforces equity and inclusion

✓ Increases participation and engagement

✓ Affirms student identity and respect

Incorporating Student Interests

Purpose:

To make learning more relevant and engaging by connecting classroom content to students' hobbies, passions, and real-world experiences.

Description:

This strategy involves weaving in students' interests—whether through examples, projects, or discussions—to create a classroom culture where learning feels meaningful and inclusive. When students see their lives reflected in lessons, they are more likely to engage deeply and retain new knowledge.

How to Use It:

1. **Get to Know Your Students**

   Learn about students' interests through surveys, morning meetings, journals, or informal conversations. Pay attention to what excites them both inside and outside of school.

2. **Integrate Interests into Lessons**

   Connect new content to what students care about. Use their hobbies and interests in examples, writing prompts, or projects tied to their passions.

3. **Invite Students to Share Expertise**

   Give students opportunities to teach or explain something they love to the class. This builds confidence and validates their unique knowledge.

4. **Keep It Ongoing**

   Revisit interests regularly and update examples as students grow and change. Rotate references so all students feel represented over time.

Example: In a math lesson on percentages, you say, "Sam, since you love basketball, let's think about free throws. If you made eight out of ten shots, what percentage would that be?" This personal connection keeps Sam engaged and makes the concept more relatable.

When to Use It:

- When introducing new or abstract concepts
- During discussions, examples, or writing prompts
- To motivate reluctant learners
- While designing projects or personalized assignments

Why It Works:

✓ Increases relevance and motivation

✓ Builds stronger teacher-student relationships

✓ Validates student identities and passions

✓ Promotes active participation and deeper learning

Sharing About Yourself

Purpose:

To build trust and connection by letting students see the person behind the role of "teacher."

Description:

This strategy involves sharing bits of your own experiences—whether connected to the lesson, a challenge you faced, or a personal interest—to humanize yourself. Sharing small, appropriate stories makes you more relatable. This creates a bridge between you and your students, fostering mutual respect and a sense of community.

How to Use It:

1. Choose Relevant Stories

Pick short anecdotes that connect to the lesson, a classroom moment, or student interests. Focus on experiences students can relate to.

2. Be Brief and Positive

Keep stories lighthearted, encouraging, or reflective and avoid making them too long or overly detailed.

3. Create Space for Students to Share

After telling a story, invite students to connect:

- "Has that ever happened to you?"
- "What do you enjoy?"

4. Be Mindful of Boundaries

Keep content age-appropriate and avoid overly private or sensitive details.

Example: During a STEM project, you say, "When I was your age, I loved building model airplanes. Watching you design your bridge reminds me of how exciting it feels to figure out how things work." This sparks students to share their own building experiences and deepens classroom connection.

When to Use It:

- When introducing new topics
- During relationship-building moments
- To make lessons more engaging and personal
- As part of fostering community and mutual respect

Why It Works:

✓ Builds authenticity and trust

✓ Strengthens teacher-student relationships

✓ Creates relatable entry points for learning

✓ Encourages students to share their own experiences

Active Listening

Purpose:

To build trust and connection by giving students your full attention.

Description:

This strategy involves giving students your full, focused attention to show that their thoughts, feelings, and experiences matter. More than hearing words, it demonstrates care and respect by being fully present, clarifying understanding, and responding thoughtfully. This simple yet powerful move strengthens relationships and creates a classroom culture of empathy.

How to Use It:

1. Be Fully Present

Stop what you're doing, make eye contact, and use open body language to signal you're fully engaged. Face the student, lean in slightly, and nod to show attentiveness.

2. Avoid Interrupting

Let the student finish their thoughts without rushing or completing sentences for them. Resist the urge to multitask.

3. Reflect and Clarify

Restate and summarize what you heard to confirm understanding. Use phrases like:

- "So, you're saying..."
- "It sounds like you're feeling..."
- "Let me check if I understood you correctly..."

4. Respond Supportively

Validate feelings before moving to solutions. Use a calm, nonjudgmental tone:

- "I can see this is frustrating for you. Let's figure it out together."

Example: After lunch, a student says they're stressed about homework. You listen quietly and reflect: "It sounds like you're feeling overwhelmed. Let's look at your planner and break it into smaller steps." The student feels supported and leaves with a plan.

When to Use It:

- During student check-ins
- In conflict resolution conversations
- When students share worries or struggles
- When students express excitement or pride
- Anytime a student approaches you to talk

Why It Works:

- ✓ Builds trust and rapport
- ✓ Validates students' feelings
- ✓ Improves communication and understanding
- ✓ Creates a safe, supportive classroom culture

Using Humor

Purpose:

To create a relaxed, engaging classroom environment where students feel comfortable, connected, and ready to learn.

Description:

This strategy involves weaving humor thoughtfully into lessons to lighten the mood, foster positive relationships, and draw students into the learning process. It's not about being a comedian; it's about adding playful, relevant moments that connect with students and enhance instruction. Humor helps reduce anxiety, build rapport, and make lessons more memorable.

How to Use It:

1. Share Relatable, Lesson-Connected Humor

Use funny examples, playful exaggerations, or gentle jokes that tie into your content. Humor works best when it's relevant to the material or relatable to students' experiences.

2. Use Playful Gestures or Actions

Add humor through tone, facial expressions, or dramatization—for example, acting surprised at a predictable outcome.

3. Defuse Tension with Lightness

Ease stress during challenging lessons or moments of frustration by using humor to reset the classroom climate.

4. Keep It Positive and Inclusive

Avoid sarcasm, embarrassment, or jokes at anyone's expense. Focus on shared laughter that brings the class together.

5. Know Your Students

Tailor humor to your students' age, personalities, and classroom culture so it feels natural and supportive.

Example: During a science lesson on gravity, you drop a pen dramatically and say, "Oh no! Gravity got me again!" The class laughs, and the playful moment reinforces the concept in a lighthearted way.

When to Use It:

- To energize the classroom when students seem tired or disengaged
- To spark curiosity and make lessons more memorable
- To reduce anxiety during tests or difficult topics
- To build classroom community through shared laughter

Why It Works:

- ✓ Builds rapport and connection
- ✓ Makes learning enjoyable and memorable
- ✓ Reduces stress and resets focus
- ✓ Encourages participation in a safe, positive way

Positive Reinforcement

Purpose:

To encourage and strengthen positive behaviors that meet classroom expectations and promote a respectful, engaged learning environment.

Description:

This strategy involves acknowledging students' efforts, choices, and contributions. Positive reinforcement helps students recognize what success looks like and motivates them to continue making good choices and repeat desired behaviors.

How to Use It:

1. **Be Specific with Praise**

   Highlight the exact behavior you want to reinforce, such as teamwork, effort, kindness, or focus. Avoid generic praise like "Good job." Instead, say things like:

   - "I noticed you stayed focused and finished your draft—that shows persistence."

2. **Use Verbal or Written Acknowledgment**

   Offer reinforcement aloud, through notes, quick messages home, or class shout-outs. Mix public and private recognition depending on the student and situation.

3. **Recognize Consistent Positive Behavior**

   Celebrate students who regularly model expectations with privileges, classroom responsibilities, or simple recognition.

4. **Make It Part of the Routine**

   Make reinforcement part of daily interactions so that all students hear what they're doing well—not just those who stand out.

Example: At the end of class, you say, "Thank you for helping clean up the art supplies, Malia. That was thoughtful and made our transition smoother." This specific, sincere acknowledgment reinforces Malia's behavior and signals to others that helpfulness is valued.

When to Use It:

- During academic tasks
- To promote classroom routines
- For encouraging appropriate social interactions
- Anytime students demonstrate behaviors that align with classroom expectations

Why It Works:

✓ Motivates students by recognizing effort and progress

✓ Reinforces classroom norms and expectations

✓ Builds confidence and self-esteem

✓ Creates a positive, supportive learning environment

"What's Working?" Conversations

Purpose:

To help students reflect on their strengths and successes so they recognize their progress, build confidence, and develop a growth mindset.

Description:

This strategy involves engaging students in reflective conversations focused on their own successes, strengths, and strategies. It guides students to notice what's already working. By focusing on what's going well, you empower students to see themselves as capable learners—even during challenges. These reflective check-ins help students develop a forward-looking mindset that supports resilience and motivation.

How to Use It:

1. Ask Positive, Reflective Questions

Use prompts such as:

- "What's working well for you in this class right now?"
- "What's something you're proud of this week?"
- "What did you do today that helped you learn?"

2. Listen and Validate

Allow students time to reflect before answering. Listen actively and affirm their responses with specific, encouraging feedback.

3. Build on Their Responses

Use what students share to guide instruction, celebrate progress, or connect their strategies to future learning. Highlight these moments as building blocks for continued growth.

4. Make It Routine

Incorporate these conversations into conferences, check-ins, or reflections so students regularly practice noticing their own growth.

Example: During a writing conference, a student feels frustrated with revisions. You ask, "What's one part of your writing you feel good about so far?" The student says, "I like my opening sentence—it really grabs attention." You respond, "You're right—that's a strong lead. Let's build the rest of your paragraph with that same energy." This reframing helps the student continue with confidence.

When to Use It:

- During one-on-one or small group conferences
- After challenging moments or setbacks
- At the end of a lesson or week
- As part of regular self-reflection routines

Why It Works:

✓ Shifts focus from deficits to strengths

✓ Encourages ownership of learning

✓ Builds confidence and resilience

✓ Reinforces positive progress and momentum

Highlighting Strengths

Purpose:

To build student confidence, foster motivation, and promote a strengths-based classroom culture.

Description:

This strategy involves recognizing and celebrating each student's unique abilities—academic, social, creative, or behavioral—to help them see their value and encourage meaningful contributions. Highlighting strengths shifts the focus from what students lack to what they bring to the classroom. By naming, affirming, and leveraging these strengths, you create an environment where all students feel capable, appreciated, and motivated to grow.

How to Use It:

1. **Notice Individual Strengths**

   Pay attention to each student's unique qualities—whether it's persistence, creativity, empathy, problem-solving, or leadership.

2. **Give Specific, Genuine Feedback**

   Point out strengths with clear, authentic comments. Decide whether to share them privately or publicly depending on the student's comfort level.

3. **Encourage Students to Use Their Strengths**

   Create opportunities for students to apply their abilities—supporting peers, leading activities, or tackling challenges in ways that highlight what they do well.

4. **Make It an Ongoing Practice**

   Intentionally look for strengths in all students, not just those who excel academically. This ensures every student feels valued.

Example: **During recess line-up, you say, "Aaliyah, I appreciate how you include everyone when you play games outside. Your kindness makes our classroom community stronger." This not only validates Aaliyah's social strength but also encourages her to keep modeling inclusion.**

When to Use It:

- During lessons and group work
- While giving individual or class feedback
- In one-on-one conferences or check-ins
- Anytime you want to build motivation, belonging, or confidence

Why It Works:

✓ Shifts focus from deficits to strengths

✓ Builds self-worth and motivation

✓ Encourages growth mindset and resilience

✓ Strengthens classroom relationships and community

Celebrating Successes

Purpose:

To build confidence, foster motivation, and reinforce a growth mindset by acknowledging both academic and personal achievements.

Description:

This strategy involves recognizing moments of success to help students see the link between effort and growth. When you celebrate achievements authentically, students feel proud, motivated, and more willing to take risks in their learning. Celebrating successes also creates a classroom culture where effort, progress, and accomplishments—big or small—are valued and noticed.

How to Use It:

1. Recognize a Range of Successes

Celebrate academic progress, positive behavior, teamwork, and social-emotional growth—not just high grades.

2. Make It Meaningful

Use specific, genuine praise that highlights *what* the student did well and *why* it matters. Tailor the recognition to fit the student and the moment.

3. Choose the Right Format

Celebrate in ways that fit your classroom:

- Verbal praise (individual or whole class)
- A success board or shout-out wall
- Certificates, notes home, or positive phone calls
- Peer-to-peer celebrations or shout-outs

Encourage Peer Recognition

Invite students to celebrate each other's achievements, building empathy, respect, and a sense of belonging.

Example: At the end of the day, you ask, "Who noticed a classmate doing something you'd like to shout-out today?"

One student says: "I want to give a shout-out to Javier because he helped me figure out the math problem when I was stuck."

Another adds: "Shout-out to Amina for including me in the basketball game at recess."

The class claps or snaps after each share.

When to Use It:

- After lessons, projects, or discussions
- When students show persistence, effort, or growth
- During community-building activities
- Anytime small wins or big accomplishments occur

Why It Works:

✓ Builds confidence and resilience
✓ Reinforces the value of effort and growth
✓ Creates a positive, supportive classroom climate
✓ Encourages risk-taking and active participation

Two-by-Ten Strategy

Purpose:

To strengthen relationships with individual students by creating consistent, positive, non-academic interactions.

Description:

This strategy involves spending two minutes a day for ten consecutive days talking casually with a student to build trust, show genuine care, and shift the dynamic from teacher–student to human–human. It is especially powerful for students who are disengaged, resistant, or struggling socially or emotionally. These intentional connections often lead to improved behavior, stronger participation, and a more inclusive classroom climate.

How to Use It:

1. Identify a Student

Select a student who would benefit from increased positive attention; someone who seems distant, unfocused, or withdrawn.

2. Start Small Conversations

Spend about two minutes each day chatting about non-academic topics like hobbies, family, favorite shows, music, or sports. Keep it light and student-centered.

3. Be Consistent and Genuine

Approach each interaction with authentic curiosity. The key is showing up every day for ten days without fail.

4. Notice Positive Shifts

Pay attention to changes in behavior, engagement, or attitude. Even subtle signs—like more eye contact, smiles, or participation—signal growing trust.

Example: Each morning for ten days, you chat with a student about their favorite basketball team—asking about games, players, and season predictions. By the end of the two weeks, you notice the student greets you with a smile, makes small talk, and begins contributing more during class.

When to Use It:

- To build or repair relationships with students who feel disconnected
- When addressing behavior challenges that stem from lack of trust
- As part of creating a welcoming, inclusive classroom culture

Why It Works:

✓ Builds consistency and trust

✓ Humanizes the teacher-student relationship

✓ Reduces behavior issues

✓ Supports long-term student engagement and belonging

Restorative Circles

Purpose:

To resolve conflicts, repair harm, and strengthen classroom community by creating a safe, respectful space for dialogue.

Description:

This strategy involves sitting together in a circle to emphasize equality and community. With clear guidelines and structured prompts, students reflect on what happened, express their feelings, and work together toward repair. This practice shifts the focus from punishment to accountability and restoration. Restorative circles help students share perspectives, listen actively, and collaborate on solutions that rebuild trust.

How to Use It:

1. Gather in a Circle

Arrange students in a circle so everyone can see and hear one another. Use this setup to signal openness and shared responsibility.

2. Set Clear Guidelines

Establish norms such as respectful listening, no interrupting, and confidentiality (when appropriate). Use a talking piece, if needed, so each student has a chance to speak.

3. Use Thoughtful Prompts

Ask questions that encourage reflection and responsibility, such as:

- "What happened from your perspective?"
- "How did this situation affect you or others?"
- "What can we do to fix this or make things right?"
- "What can we learn from this experience as a group?"

4. **Ensure All Voices Are Heard**

   Give everyone an opportunity to contribute while respecting the choice to pass. Emphasize empathy, patience, and understanding.

5. **Collaborate on Solutions**

   Focus on repairing relationships and developing actionable next steps that all participants agree upon.

Example: After a conflict at recess, you bring the involved students together in a circle. Each shares their perspective and listens as others speak. Together, the group agrees on a plan for moving forward, including an apology, new ground rules for games, and a commitment to check in with each other.

When to Use It:

- After conflicts or misunderstandings
- To address harm and rebuild relationships
- Proactively, as part of regular classroom community-building

Why It Works:

✓ Promotes accountability over punishment

✓ Builds empathy and listening skills

✓ Strengthens community bonds and trust

Community Circles

Purpose:

To foster classroom connection, empathy, and belonging by creating a structured space for sharing and reflection.

Description:

This strategy involves gathering in a circle to encourage equality, openness, and inclusion. With clear norms and open-ended prompts, students can listen, share, and support one another. Community circles strengthen classroom culture and help students feel part of something bigger.

How to Use It:

1. **Set the Tone**

   Establish expectations for respectful listening, one speaker at a time, and no judgment. Use a talking piece to signal whose turn it is.

2. **Choose a Focus**

   Use community circles for a variety of purposes, such as:

   - Morning check-ins
   - Celebrations and shout-outs
   - Class problem-solving
   - Reflecting on lessons or group work
   - Practicing social-emotional skills

3. **Use Open-Ended Prompts**

   Guide the conversation with prompts like:

   - "What's one thing you're proud of this week?"
   - "How can we support each other today?"
   - "What's one way we can fix this together?"

4. **Encourage Participation Without Pressure**

   Allow students to pass if they don't feel ready to share. Focus on inclusion and respect, not forcing responses.

5. **Close with Positivity**

   End circles with a unifying message, reflection, or affirmation that carries the positive tone into the rest of the day.

Example: On Monday morning, you begin a community circle with: "Share one thing you're looking forward to this week, or one goal you have." Each student shares while others listen. You close with a group affirmation: "We are ready for a great week!"

When to Use It:

- As part of daily or weekly classroom routines
- When seeking student input
- For problem-solving classroom issues
- To share appreciations

Why It Works:

✓ Builds community and belonging

✓ Strengthens listening and empathy

✓ Creates a safe, supportive classroom community

✓ Encourages ownership of the learning environment

Final Thoughts

The strongest relationships in the classroom aren't built in big, dramatic moments—they're built in the small, steady ones. The *good mornings*. The patient redirection. The quiet *I'm glad you're here*.

When students feel connected to you, they try harder. They trust more. They open up. And that changes everything. Not just the way they learn, but the way they see themselves.

Your classroom is more than a place where learning happens. It's a place where kids are known, respected, and cared for. Every relationship-building move you make reinforces that truth.

So, keep showing up. Keep noticing. Keep connecting. You're not just teaching students. You're shaping how they experience school—and how they carry themselves into the world.

Up Next

Once students trust you and feel safe in your classroom, the next step is to invite them into the learning in ways that spark curiosity, excitement, and investment. That's where engagement moves come in.

In the next chapter, we'll look at high-impact engagement moves that build on these relationships—because when students feel seen, they're ready to be drawn in.

PUTTING IT INTO PRACTICE

Now that you've seen the why and how behind effective relationship-building moves, let's explore what they might look like in real life.

The following scenarios are pulled from common classroom moments—ones that every teacher has faced in some form. Each one invites you to pause, reflect, and consider:

What moves would I make in this moment?

This is where theory meets practice—where your instincts and toolkit come together.

SCENARIOS

The Crumpled Picture

The Invisible Student

The Reading Rebellion

Scenario 1: The Crumpled Picture

It's early in the school year in your grade 2 classroom. You're finishing up an activity where students were asked to draw something that makes them feel happy. Most students are eagerly showing their drawings with smiling stick figures, sunny skies, favorite pets.

But Liam, who's been quiet and reserved since the first day, sits at his desk staring at a crumpled paper in his hand.

You walk over and kneel beside him.

"Do you want to show me your picture?" you ask gently.

He shakes his head.

"Mine's dumb."

You offer a calm smile:

"I bet it's not. I'd love to see it."

Liam sighs, hesitates, then flattens the paper on the desk. It's a shaky drawing of a broken toy car and a stick figure with tears.

You say softly, "Is that your toy?"

He nods, eyes down. Then adds: "My dad threw it out when he got mad."

You pause, heart catching a little at the unexpected honesty.

The bell rings. The moment could slip away.

You have twenty other students to get outside for recess.

But this moment matters. It's not about the picture. It's about Liam telling you something—without saying it.

How Might You Respond?

- How can you respond in a way that builds safety and trust with Liam?
- What relationship-building moves might create space for connection without making him feel exposed?
- How do you balance this one quiet moment with the busyness of the classroom around you?

Scenario 2: The Invisible Student

It's mid-October, and you're finally finding your rhythm with your grade 7 class. Most students are engaged, routines are sticking, and the class has a good energy overall.

Except for Maya.

Maya is quiet. Always. She comes in, sits in the back, does her work (usually), and rarely speaks unless called on directly. She doesn't cause problems, but she doesn't really connect with peers or with you.

You've tried a few casual conversations at the door and commented on her drawings once or twice, but she mostly shrugs and avoids eye contact.

Today, while the class is working on a group poster project, Maya sits alone. She says she prefers it that way. When you ask how it's going, she says, "Fine." But you notice her paper is mostly blank.

As you move away to check on another group, you hear a student mutter, "Why is she even here if she's not gonna do anything?"

Maya pretends not to hear. But you see her shoulders tense.

You pause. You have a choice:

- Brush it off and keep things moving.
- Step in and address the comment.
- Circle back later.

You realize this isn't just about a group project.

It's about whether Maya feels like she belongs here.

How Might You Respond?

- How could you use this moment to build trust with Maya?
- What relationship-building moves might help her feel seen and valued?
- How can you shape a classroom culture where every student feels they matter?

Scenario 3: The Reading Rebellion

It's mid-morning in your grade 6 classroom. The students have just come back from gym, sweaty, chatty, and slightly wound up. You signal for the class to transition into independent reading time—lights dimmed, soft music on, a calm reset.

Most students settle in. Except for Riley.

Riley drops into his chair with a loud *thud* and immediately kicks his backpack across the floor. His book sits untouched on the desk. You approach quietly and say, "Let's get started on reading, Riley. It's time."

He doesn't even look at you. His arms are folded, jaw tight.

You offer a choice: "Would you rather read here or take your book to the back table?"

That's when things erupt. Riley shoves the book off his desk with both hands. It hits the floor with a slap.

"I'M NOT DOING IT!" he shouts.

Heads snap up across the room. A few students freeze. One quietly says, "Whoa."

You feel the air go still. You take a slow breath, keeping your voice steady as you try again: "I can see you're upset. Let's talk about it."

Riley cuts you off: "No. Just leave me alone. You're always on me. I don't care about this stupid class."

You know Riley's been struggling lately—missing homework, frequent outbursts, eye rolling, and disengagement. But now, all eyes are on you.

Do you push forward? Give space? Call for support?

This is one of those moments that could define your relationship with Riley—for better or worse.

How Might You Respond?

- How would you de-escalate this moment while maintaining boundaries and classroom safety?
- How might your response affect Riley—and the rest of the class?
- What proactive moves might shift this dynamic in the future?

Chapter 5

Engagement Moves

"When we get to talk to each other about what we're learning, I remember it better." **—Grade 4 student**

Engagement is the bridge between attention and understanding.

Even the best lesson plan can fall flat if students aren't drawn in. When students are actively involved—when they're talking, trying, wondering, building, connecting—they learn more, remember more, and feel more invested. That's the power of engagement moves.

They turn passive listeners into active learners.

Why These Moves Matter

Engagement is about helping students stay connected to the *why* behind the learning. When students are engaged, they're more likely to think deeply, try harder, and stick with a task—even when it's tough.

Strong engagement moves allow you to:

- Spark curiosity and excitement around the curriculum content.
- Minimize disruptions by maximizing focus.
- Reach learners with different strengths, needs, and interests.
- Build a culture where students want to participate.
- Help students make personal connections that deepen understanding.

An intentional question, a hands-on task, or a real-world connection can turn a distracted student into an invested learner.

So, What Are Engagement Moves?

Engagement moves are the intentional choices you make—before and during instruction—to make learning feel relevant, exciting, and worth your students' time. Some are built into your planning, like designing a problem-based learning opportunity or choosing a great read aloud. Others happen in the moment, like using a callback to refocus the group or turning a student response into a teachable moment.

Think of them as your "hook and hold" strategies. They help you draw students in, keep energy high, and make the learning experience one students want to be involved in.

Engagement moves are about meaningful involvement.

Inviting Students into the Learning Process

As a learning support teacher, I had the privilege of delivering the Empower Reading Program to small groups of struggling readers each day. The program was research-based, structured, and built for students who needed explicit, direct instruction to learn how to read.

And over the years, it worked. Our students experienced real success—gaining skills, confidence, and the belief that they were readers.

Then came Kenny.

Kenny was different. No matter how clearly I taught the lessons or how consistently we followed routines, Kenny struggled. Each day began with his head on the table and a whisper: "I can't read."

Occasionally, his head would lift when he recognized a word or had a moment of confidence, and he'd participate. But when we reached the final part of each lesson—a short decodable story—he would shut down again. He couldn't yet transfer strategies to his reading.

I had a decision to make. I could stick with the program, or I could veer from the plan and meet Kenny where he was, inviting him back into the learning process.

I chose the latter.

I gave Kenny full autonomy to choose any story, even one from earlier lessons. He chose the very first one—a three-sentence story with a simple pattern.

He read it again. And again. And again.

Then one day, he turned the page. He tried the second story—and he could decode it.

"Can I read it to you?" he asked excitedly.

"Of course," I said. Then gently asked: "Would you like to read it to the group also?"

He hesitated. Then nodded.

He read the entire short story aloud. When he finished, the group burst into applause. Kenny beamed.

From that day forward, something shifted. He began to take more risks. He started trying new stories—even when they were hard. And when the frustration crept back in, he'd flip back to a story he knew well and reread it. I saw this not as regression, but as a **self-regulation strategy**. His way of protecting his own emotional safety while staying engaged.

Slowly, his confidence grew. He started asking to read to other teachers. Then, one day, he asked to read to his entire class.

He sat on the carpet, book in hand, and read a story in front of his peers. When he finished, he ran across the room and gave me the biggest hug.

"Thank you for teaching me to read."

That might have been the best moment of my twenty-five-year teaching career. Finally, Kenny saw himself as a reader!

That moment didn't come from following the script. It came from adjusting the move—to re-engage a student who needed a new way in.

What Makes These Moves Work?

Engagement moves are about invitation.

At their core, these moves draw students into the learning process and help them stay there. They create energy, spark curiosity, and make learning feel alive. When students are engaged, they're not just paying attention. They're investing effort, emotion, and thought. And that's where the deeper learning happens.

Here's what strong engagement moves do:

Spark Interest

A good hook can change everything. Whether it's a surprising fact, a compelling story, or a mystery that begs to be solved, engagement starts when students want to know more.

Encourage Participation

Students don't learn by watching. They learn by doing. Whether it's a debate, a hands-on task, or a tech-based tool, engagement moves bring students into the action.

Build Intrinsic Motivation

When students understand why the learning matters to their lives, their goals, or the bigger world—they're more likely to care. That internal "why" drives deeper commitment.

Support Focus and Attention

Variety keeps attention sharp. By shifting the pace, format, or activity, you help students stay with you from start to finish—even when the content gets challenging.

Create Emotional Buy-In

When students feel safe, involved, and excited, they lean in more fully. Emotional connection fuels effort, persistence, and joy in learning.

In addition, the most effective engagement moves are:

- **Purposeful** – The activity serves a clear learning goal.
- **Interactive** – Students are doing, talking, solving.
- **Relevant** – Learning connects to real life or personal interests.
- **Varied** – A balance of novelty and predictability keeps students interested.
- **Inclusive** – Everyone has a way in—no matter their style or pace.
- **Sustainable** – The strategy works for you too. If it drains you, it won't last.

When these elements are in place, your classroom becomes a place students want to be. A space where learning feels active, exciting, and worth showing up for.

Real Talk: What This Looks Like in Action

You're teaching about the water cycle. It's midweek. The room feels flat.

What do you do?

- You start with a call-and-response chant—***callback move.***
- You set up a mystery: "A puddle appeared on a sunny day. What happened?"— ***build anticipation move.***
- You read a story about a rainy day with drama and suspense—***read-aloud move.***
- You pause for students to act out a fun part—***movement move.***
- You end with a personal connection: "How does the weather affect us?"—***real-world connection move.***

In fifteen minutes, you've turned a flat moment into active learning. Students are hooked.

That's what intentional engagement looks like.

You Don't Have to Do It All at Once

Great teaching isn't about using every strategy. It's about choosing a strategy with intention.

Start small and build from there:

- Try a call-and-response to bring attention back before giving directions.
- Add a real-world connection to one lesson each day.
- Include a hands-on task once a week to boost participation.
- Kick off a new unit by reading aloud to spark curiosity.

Small shifts can spark big engagement.

Let's Explore: 12 Engagement Moves

On the following pages, we'll dive into twelve teacher moves that bring learning to life, boost student motivation, and help create a classroom students can't wait to be part of:

Callbacks and Chants
Building Anticipation
Reading Aloud
Student-Led Learning
Peer Collaboration
Class Debates
Cold Calling
Hands-On Activities
Gamification
Real-World Connections
Problem-Based Learning
Technology and Interactive Media

Let's take a closer look at each.

Callbacks and Chants

Purpose:

To quickly capture students' attention, manage transitions, and re-energize the class in a playful yet predictable way.

Description:

This strategy involves using short, rhythmic phrases or repeat-after-me responses to signal students to stop, listen, and refocus. Callbacks and chants reduce the need to raise your voice and increase engagement through rhythm, novelty, and routine. When used consistently, they provide a fun and effective structure for managing classroom transitions and regaining attention.

How to Use It:

1. Teach and Practice

Introduce a callback phrase and model the expected student response. Practice together until it becomes automatic.

2. Use for Transitions and Refocusing

Use callbacks when moving between activities, after group work, or when noise levels rise. They signal, "Eyes on me," without raising your voice.

3. Keep It Fresh

Rotate phrases, add motions, or tie chants to classroom themes. Invite students to suggest ideas to boost buy-in.

4. Be Consistent

Deliver the call-back with the same rhythm and tone each time so students learn to respond immediately.

Example:

You say: "Hocus pocus!"

Students: "Everybody focus!"

(Students stop what they're doing, repeat the phrase, and turn their attention to you.)

When to Use It:

- To start lessons or signal readiness
- During transitions
- To regain attention when energy rises
- To re-energize focus when students drift

Why It Works:

✓ Provides a playful, low-stress attention signal

✓ Builds routine and consistency

✓ Engages students actively in classroom management

Building Anticipation

Purpose:

To spark curiosity and excitement so students are motivated to dive into the lesson.

Description:

This strategy involves presenting students with puzzles, questions, or scenarios that don't have an immediate answer. By creating intrigue or mystery, you engage their natural desire to explore, predict, and solve problems. This approach primes their brains for active participation and builds buy-in for the learning ahead.

How to Use It:

1. **Set the Hook**

   Begin with a surprising fact, puzzling question, unusual image, or real-world scenario that ties into your lesson. Leave just enough mystery to spark the question, "What's next?"

2. **Drop Clues Along the Way**

   Provide hints, partial information, or small reveals throughout the lesson. This keeps curiosity high and encourages deeper critical thinking.

3. **Encourage Collaborative Thinking**

   Ask students to predict, brainstorm, or problem-solve in pairs or groups. Shared curiosity builds momentum and amplifies engagement.

4. **Reveal the Connection**

   Lead students toward the solution and connect it back to the learning goal. Highlight how the sense of anticipation made the content more meaningful.

Example: At the start of a lesson on probability, you pull out a jar of mixed candies and say, "If I reach in without looking, what's the chance I'll grab a red one?" Students make predictions, then work through probability concepts to test their guesses.

When to Use It:

- At the beginning of lessons to hook attention
- During inquiry-based or project-based learning
- When reviewing material in a challenge or game format
- In any subject where curiosity can fuel deeper engagement

Why It Works:

✓ Activates curiosity and critical thinking
✓ Makes learning feel like discovery rather than a task
✓ Creates emotional investment in the outcome

Reading Aloud

Purpose:

To engage students, model fluent reading, and make content more meaningful and accessible.

Description:

This strategy involves reading aloud to students to bring text to life in a way that encourages listening comprehension and curiosity. Through expressive delivery and purposeful pauses, you show students how readers think, question, and connect with what they read. Reading aloud captures attention, supports comprehension, and creates shared learning experiences that help students connect emotionally and intellectually to the material.

How to Use It:

1. Choose Purposeful Texts

Select age-appropriate, engaging texts that align with your learning goals. These might include picture books, biographies, news articles, poems, or excerpts from novels.

2. Set the Stage

Introduce the text with a brief hook or context to spark interest and explain why you're reading it.

3. Read with Expression

Use tone, pacing, and emphasis to highlight emotion, suspense, humor, or dialogue.

4. Pause to Interact

Stop occasionally to:

- Ask questions and check for understanding
- Predict outcomes
- Clarify new vocabulary
- Connect to prior knowledge or real life

5. **Extend the Learning**

   Guide a discussion, reflection, or quick task that links the text back to your learning goal.

Example: **In science class, you read aloud a short article about astronauts training for space missions. As you pause, students predict what challenges astronauts might face in zero gravity and connect the information to their own upcoming science experiment on forces and motion.**

When to Use It:

- Across subjects to introduce new concepts or themes
- To model fluent and expressive reading
- To create a shared classroom experience
- For social-emotional learning

Why It Works:

✓ Creates engagement through storytelling
✓ Builds background knowledge and empathy
✓ Builds vocabulary and comprehension skills
✓ Strengthens listening skills and attention

Student-Led Learning

Purpose:

To give students ownership of learning by connecting their outside experiences, skills, and passions to classroom activities.

Description:

This strategy involves allowing students to share their knowledge, talents, or strategies with peers. By integrating personal expertise into lessons, you create a richer classroom environment where students both teach and learn from one another. This approach fosters confidence, collaboration, and deeper connections to the curriculum.

How to Use It:

1. **Discover Student Skills and Interests**

   Use surveys, conversations, or journal prompts to uncover students' hobbies, talents, or personal passions.

2. **Create Opportunities to Share**

   Build in moments for students to present, model, or demonstrate their knowledge during lessons, projects, or discussions.

3. **Connect to Learning Goals**

   Show how their contributions link to the curriculum, helping students see the relevance of their experiences to academic learning.

4. **Encourage Peer Learning**

   Facilitate spaces where students can teach classmates new strategies or approaches, building respect and collaboration.

Example: During a visual arts unit on shading and texture, a student who practices anime-style drawing at home shares her sketchbook and demonstrates how she uses cross-hatching for depth. The class experiments with the technique in their own work, expanding their artistic toolkit.

When to Use It:

- Across all subject areas
- When a student has unique skills or experiences that relate to curriculum content

Why It Works:

- ✓ Builds student confidence and leadership
- ✓ Makes learning more meaningful
- ✓ Highlights students' diverse strengths and perspectives

Peer Collaboration

Purpose:

To provide students with opportunities to learn from one another, share perspectives, and solve problems together.

Description:

This strategy involves allowing students to work together on structured tasks that require cooperation and multiple viewpoints. By engaging in shared problem-solving, discussion, and creative work, students develop both academic understanding and social-emotional skills. Collaboration builds communication, teamwork, and critical-thinking skills while strengthening classroom community.

How to Use It:

1. Design Collaborative Tasks

Plan activities that can't be completed effectively alone—such as debates, STEM challenges, group problem-solving, or shared writing tasks.

2. Assign Roles

Give each student a role (e.g., Reader, Recorder, Questioner, Summarizer, or Materials Manager) to ensure balanced participation. Rotate roles regularly so everyone practices different skills.

3. Teach Collaboration Skills

Explicitly model and practice how to:

- Take turns speaking
- Listen actively
- Disagree respectfully
- Make decisions as a team

4. **Monitor and Support**

   Circulate while groups are working. Observe participation, encourage respectful interaction, and coach students through conflict or off-task behavior.

5. **Reflect and Debrief**

   After the activity, ask students to reflect on both the academic task and their teamwork. Use prompts like:

   - "What went well in your group?"
   - "What could we improve next time?"

Example: During a nature walk, each student in the group has a specific role. One student is the **Observer**, pointing out plants or animals they notice. Another is the **Recorder**, drawing or writing notes on a clipboard. A third is the **Collector**, gathering safe items like leaves or small rocks. A fourth is the **Questioner**, asking things like, "Why do you think this plant grows here?" After the walk, the group shares their findings by combining everyone's contributions into a poster about their discoveries.

When to Use It:

- During project-based learning or problem-solving activities
- In discussions where multiple viewpoints strengthen understanding
- To deepen engagement and build classroom community

Why It Works:

✓ Strengthens critical thinking through multiple perspectives

✓ Builds social-emotional, communication, and leadership skills

✓ Creates a supportive, community-driven classroom culture

Class Debates

Purpose:

To give students opportunities to express opinions, defend ideas with evidence, and engage with multiple viewpoints.

Description:

This strategy involves having students take different positions on a debatable topic and use research, reasoning, and evidence to defend their claims. It promotes active listening, respectful disagreement, and engagement with real-world issues. Class debates develop critical thinking, persuasive communication, and civil dialogue, making learning interactive and relevant.

How to Use It:

1. Select a Relevant Topic

Choose a topic that connects to your curriculum or current events. Ensure it has clear, debatable sides (e.g., "Should homework be mandatory?" or "Is technology helping or harming communication?").

2. Assign Positions

Divide students into groups representing different perspectives. Depending on your goal, you can assign roles or let students choose.

3. Establish Ground Rules

Model and reinforce expectations such as:

- Listen actively without interrupting
- Disagree with ideas, not people
- Use evidence to back up opinions
- Speak respectfully and clearly

4. Prepare Arguments

Give students time to research, write talking points, and collaborate within their groups before the debate begins.

5. **Facilitate the Debate**

   Moderate by keeping time, prompting quieter voices to join, and ensuring balance between sides. Offer sentence starters to support participation if needed.

6. **Debrief and Reflect**

   Guide students to reflect on what they learned about the issue, how they communicated, and what strategies made the debate effective.

Example: In science class, students debate the pros and cons of renewable vs. non-renewable energy sources. One group argues for solar and wind energy, while the other emphasizes the challenges of cost, access, and storage. Students must use research-based evidence to support their claims, practicing critical thinking and real-world application.

When to Use It:

- To teach persuasive writing or public speaking
- During lessons that involve complex, real-world issues
- To deepen critical thinking and analysis of multiple perspectives
- To practice respectful disagreement and collaborative dialogue

Why It Works:

✓ Builds confidence in public speaking

✓ Teaches evidence-based reasoning

✓ Promotes respectful communication and empathy

✓ Fosters emotional buy-in

Cold Calling

Purpose:

To keep all students engaged, accountable, and ready to participate by calling on them randomly or non-voluntarily.

Description:

This strategy involves posing a question to the entire class, giving students time to think, and then calling on one student to respond. This strategy promotes equity by ensuring that every student—not just the eager volunteers—has a voice in class discussions. It encourages active listening, reduces reliance on a handful of participants, and creates a culture where everyone's input is expected and valued.

How to Use It:

1. Set the Expectation

At the beginning of the year, explain that cold calling is a regular, supportive practice. Emphasize that it's about thinking together, not putting anyone on the spot.

2. Ask First, Then Call

Pose your question to the whole class and provide silent "think time" before selecting a student. This helps everyone prepare and reduces anxiety.

3. Randomize Selection

Use tools like name sticks, index cards, or a random name generator to ensure fairness and eliminate bias.

4. Support All Answers

Respond positively to student contributions, whether correct or not. Use answers as a springboard for deeper discussion, encouraging peers to add on or refine ideas.

5. **Normalize Mistakes**

   Frame incorrect answers as valuable learning opportunities. Reinforce that errors are a natural part of the learning process.

Example: During a geography lesson on Canada's physical regions, you ask, "Which landform region do the Rocky Mountains belong to?" After giving think time, you pull a popsicle stick from a jar and say, "Ava—what do you think?" Ava answers, "The Western Cordillera." You respond, "Exactly! Great recall. Let's add why the Rockies are important to Canada—who can build on Ava's answer?"

When to Use It:

- During whole-class discussions
- For content review sessions
- When introducing new material
- Any time you want students to remain engaged and accountable

Why It Works:

✓ Promotes equity by giving every student a voice

✓ Keeps all students actively thinking

✓ Reduces over-reliance on frequent volunteers

Hands-On Activities

Purpose:

To engage students in active, tactile learning by having them create, build, manipulate, or experiment with materials.

Description:

This strategy involves providing opportunities for students to learn by doing—using materials, tools, or models that make abstract concepts visible and interactive. Hands-on activities encourage exploration, critical thinking, and collaboration, making learning both memorable and meaningful. This approach helps students move from abstract concepts to concrete understanding and reinforces skills through exploration and physical involvement.

How to Use It:

1. **Design Purposeful Tasks**

   Plan activities that directly align with learning objectives. Examples include building models, conducting experiments, creating art projects, assembling timelines, or designing prototypes.

2. **Prepare Materials and Instructions**

   Provide all necessary tools and clear, step-by-step instructions. Use visual aids, demonstrations, or checklists to support students who may need extra guidance.

3. **Encourage Collaboration**

   Organize students into pairs or small groups to foster teamwork, problem-solving, and peer learning as they complete the task.

4. **Facilitate and Observe**

   Move around the room to offer support, ask guiding questions, and prompt students to explain their thinking as they work.

5. **Reflect and Connect**

   After the activity, lead a discussion or journal reflection to help students connect the experience to the learning goal. Ask prompts such as:

   - "What did you notice?"
   - "What did you learn?"
   - "How does this connect to our topic?"

Example: In science class, you ask students to work in teams to design and build a model bridge using recycled materials. After testing their bridges to see how much weight they can hold, you guide a discussion about which designs were strongest and why.

When to Use It:

- When introducing new concepts
- When reinforcing complex ideas
- During consolidation of learning
- When supporting students who learn best through kinesthetic, experiential approaches

Why It Works:

✓ Makes abstract ideas concrete

✓ Boosts engagement and retention

✓ Provides immediate feedback for formative assessment

✓ Strengthens collaboration, communication, and problem solving skills

Gamification

Purpose:

To make learning more engaging by turning lessons into games, challenges, or missions.

Description:

This strategy involves transforming regular learning activities into game-like experiences with points, challenges, rewards, or cooperative missions. By tapping into students' natural love of play, you make learning fun, interactive, and memorable. Gamification increases motivation, focus, and participation while keeping lessons tied to your curriculum goals.

How to Use It:

1. **Design Learning Games**

   Build games that align directly with your learning goals. Add points, team challenges, badges, rewards, or timed missions to reinforce content while making practice exciting.

2. **Use Interactive Tools**

   Incorporate platforms like Kahoot!, Quizizz, or Blooket—or design your own games using whiteboards, task cards, scavenger hunts, or relay races.

3. **Level the Playing Field**

   Structure games so every student can participate meaningfully. Mix ability levels in teams, award points for effort and collaboration (not just speed), and design challenges with multiple entry points for success.

4. **Track Progress**

   Use leaderboards, progress charts, or class milestones to build excitement and show growth over time.

5. **Debrief the Experience**

   After each game, reflect with students on what they learned, how they worked together, and how the activity connected to the learning goal.

Example: In geography class, you turn review into a "Race Across Canada." Each team answers trivia questions about provinces and territories. Correct answers let them move their marker across a giant map posted on the wall. The first team to "reach" the Pacific Ocean wins—but along the way, every team is reviewing key facts and practicing map skills.

When to Use It:

- During review lessons or unit wrap-ups
- For skill practice that might otherwise feel repetitive
- When students need a boost of energy or motivation
- To promote collaboration and teamwork in any subject

Why It Works:

- ✓ Increases motivation and engagement
- ✓ Strengthens memory and retention
- ✓ Builds collaboration and communication skills
- ✓ Makes routine tasks more exciting and meaningful

Real-World Connections

Purpose:

To make learning meaningful by linking academic content to students' every-day lives, interests, and current events.

Description:

This strategy involves connecting teaching to real-world contexts—through practical examples, current issues, or student experiences—so students recognize the value and relevance of what they're learning. When students see how lessons apply beyond the classroom, they gain motivation, purpose, and a deeper understanding of the material.

How to Use It:

1. Identify Relevant Connections

Find natural links between your learning goal and real-life applications, student interests, or community issues.

2. Spark Discussion

Pose guiding questions such as:

- "Where have you seen this in real life?"
- "When might you need this skill outside of school?"
- "How does this connect to something happening in the world right now?"

3. Encourage Personal Reflection

Invite students to share experiences or examples from their own lives. Validate and expand on their contributions to build ownership and engagement.

4. Use Applied Learning

Incorporate project-based learning, real-life case studies, simulations, or problem-solving activities that require students to apply academic skills in practical ways.

5. **Bring in Outside Perspectives**

   Invite guest speakers, show media clips, or plan real-world experiences (virtual or in-person) that demonstrate how the content is used beyond school.

Example: During a lesson on ratios, you bring in a recipe for chocolate chip cookies. You ask students, "If this recipe makes twenty-four cookies and we only want twelve, how should we change the ingredient amounts?" Students work in pairs to adjust the measurements, then discuss how ratios apply in everyday cooking.

When to Use It:

- When introducing abstract concepts
- To motivate reluctant learners
- When outside experts can enrich learning experiences

Why It Works:

✓ Builds relevance and meaning in learning

✓ Increases motivation by connecting content to students' lives

✓ Encourages critical thinking about real-world issues

✓ Helps students transfer knowledge and skills beyond school

Problem-Based Learning

Purpose:

To transform students from passive listeners into active problem-solvers by engaging them with authentic, real-world challenges.

Description:

This strategy involves presenting students with a complex, open-ended problem tied to your learning goals. Students take ownership of the process by brainstorming, researching, testing ideas, and collaborating to design solutions. This approach sparks curiosity, deepens understanding, and helps students see the relevance of what they're learning.

How to Use It:

1. Pose an Authentic Problem

Start with a real-world challenge or question that connects to your unit. Choose problems that are open-ended, require multiple perspectives, and invite creativity.

2. Encourage Inquiry

Let students generate questions, explore resources, and brainstorm possible solutions. Push them to use reasoning and evidence in their discussions.

3. Facilitate, Don't Direct

Step into the role of coach. Provide guiding questions, check-ins, and scaffolds while allowing students to take responsibility for the direction of their learning.

4. Share Solutions

Have students present their work through models, presentations, debates, or written proposals. Encourage them to explain not only the solution but also the process they used to get there.

Example: In geography class, you challenge students to design a sustainable city plan that addresses climate change, transportation, and housing. They research real-world innovations, collaborate in groups to design their city, and present their models to the class—defending their choices with evidence.

When to Use It:

- When you want to boost engagement and curiosity
- During cross-curricular projects that connect multiple subjects
- When reinforcing the real-world relevance of academic content

Why It Works:

✓ Builds critical thinking and problem-solving skills

✓ Encourages collaboration and communication

✓ Makes learning relevant and meaningful

✓ Promotes student ownership of the learning process

Technology and Interactive Media

Purpose:

To use digital tools and interactive platforms to increase engagement, personalize learning, and make abstract concepts more accessible.

Description:

This strategy involves using technology to bring lessons to life by helping students visualize abstract concepts, collaborate in real time, and access a wide range of digital resources. When chosen and implemented thoughtfully, interactive media creates dynamic learning experiences that support student engagement and diverse learning needs.

How to Use It:

1. Select Purposeful Tools

Choose technology that directly supports your learning goals, such as:

- Interactive simulations (e.g., virtual labs, digital manipulatives)
- Collaborative platforms (e.g., shared docs, virtual whiteboards)
- Gamified quizzes (e.g., Kahoot!, Blooket, Quizizz)
- Multimedia resources (e.g., podcasts, videos, animations)
- Assistive technology (e.g., text-to-speech apps, closed captioning)

2. Model and Teach Tech Use

Demonstrate how to use the tool step by step. Set clear expectations for digital citizenship, respectful collaboration, and staying on task.

3. Integrate Actively

Use tech to spark curiosity, promote participation, and encourage collaboration—not just passive screen time. Keep students interacting with both the content and each other.

4. **Monitor and Support**

   Move around the room to check in, troubleshoot, and ensure students stay engaged. Provide guidance as needed.

5. **Reflect and Share**

   Afterward, invite students to reflect on their learning and discuss how the tool supported their understanding.

Example: During a geography lesson, you use Google Earth to explore natural landmarks around the world. Students work in groups to "visit" assigned regions, capture screenshots, and create a shared slideshow comparing climate, culture, and geography.

When to Use It:

- Across all subject areas
- When providing targeted practice and review
- For visualizing abstract or complex concepts
- To collect real-time assessment data

Why It Works:

✓ Makes learning interactive and accessible

✓ Supports diverse learning styles and needs

✓ Extends learning beyond the classroom

✓ Builds digital literacy skills

✓ Increases engagement

Final Thoughts

Engagement moves aren't just strategies. They're how you breathe life into your lessons. When you invite students to interact, connect, and care about what they're learning, you shift the energy in your classroom. Students aren't just going through the motions—they're leaning in, asking questions, and making meaning.

As you experiment with different engagement moves, remember there's no one-size-fits-all. Some students come alive in a debate, others in a hands-on task, and still others in quiet reflection. The strength of engagement lies in variety and intention—meeting students where they are and offering multiple pathways in.

And it's not just about boosting academics (though it does that, too). When students feel engaged, they feel seen. They feel capable. They feel like what they're doing matters. That sense of connection and purpose is what builds confident, curious learners who are ready for whatever comes next.

In the end, engagement is about creating a classroom where students *want* to be—where learning feels meaningful, and where every student has the chance to grow, contribute, and thrive.

Up Next

The next challenge is ensuring that every learner, no matter their starting point, can access, process, and succeed with the content. That's where differentiation moves come in. In the next chapter, we'll explore practical strategies to tailor instruction, adjust expectations, and provide the right level of challenge and support so all students can thrive.

PUTTING IT INTO PRACTICE

Now that you've seen the why and how behind effective engagement moves, let's explore what they might look like in real life.

The following scenarios are pulled from common classroom moments—ones that every teacher has faced in some form. Each one invites you to pause, reflect, and consider:

What moves might I make in this moment?

This is where theory meets practice—and where your instincts and toolkit come together.

SCENARIOS

The One-Day Chaos

The Paragraph Writing Shutdown

Silence in French Class

Scenario 1: The One-Day Chaos

You arrive early for your one-day supply assignment in a grade 7 classroom. The plans are minimal—just a brief note that says: "Students know the routine. Here's the schedule. Good luck!"

You glance around. The classroom looks a bit disorganized with papers scattered, desks facing all directions, no visible class rules or routines posted. You shrug it off. Maybe it's just a relaxed style.

Then the bell rings.

Within minutes, it becomes clear: **this classroom runs on chaos.**

- Several students walk in late without explanation.
- Others immediately start shouting across the room, throwing paper, and arguing over chairs.
- When you ask for attention, a few students ignore you completely.
- Others laugh and say, "Our teacher lets us talk whenever we want."
- During independent work time, one student gets up and starts wandering the halls. Another student refuses to do anything, arms crossed, saying, "You're not my real teacher."

You try to redirect. You attempt to implement some basic structure.

But every request is met with resistance or complete indifference.

You look around the room and realize:

There are no expectations here. No sense of community.

And today, you're in charge.

How Might You Respond?

- How might you establish calm, safety, and structure as a guest teacher in just one day?
- What "supply teacher moves" can help you connect with students who are used to running the show?
- How do you maintain your authority while still being respectful of the space and relationships you're walking into?

Scenario 2: The Paragraph Writing Shutdown

It's a Tuesday afternoon, and you're halfway through a unit on paragraph writing with your grade 4 class. Today's goal: introduce the hamburger model to help students structure their writing more clearly.

You begin with a thorough review of the model, then display a colorful anchor chart showing topic sentence, supporting details, and conclusion. You even model a paragraph about your favorite food—pizza—with enthusiasm and detail.

But when it's time for students to begin drafting their own paragraphs...it's crickets.

Heads are down. A few kids are doodling. One is braiding another's hair. A couple of students quietly ask to go to the bathroom, and others start flipping through their notebooks aimlessly.

You give a few redirections, but nothing sticks. The engagement is flat. You feel like you're dragging the class through quicksand.

You notice:

- No one has picked up a pencil to start.
- One student whispers, "I hate writing."
- Another shrugs and says, "Can I just type it?"
- Molly glances at the clock...and so do you.

The lesson you thought would spark creativity and confidence has somehow turned into a silent protest.

How Might You Respond?

- How might you re-engage students in the moment?
- What teacher moves could shift the energy without abandoning your goal?
- Would you push through? Pivot? Pause and revisit later?

Scenario 3: Silence in French Class

It's Thursday morning, and you're teaching a grade 6 Core French class. Today's goal is to practice simple conversational phrases using the verb *avoir* (to have) in context. You've prepared a partner activity where students ask and answer questions like *"Tu as un frère?"* and *"Tu as un animal de compagnie?"*

You review the vocabulary together and model the conversation with a student volunteer. Then, you send students off to practice in pairs.

But as you circulate, you notice the classroom is...strangely quiet.

- Some students are whispering in English.
- Others aren't talking at all—just staring at their sheets.
- A few ask, "Can we just write the answers instead?"
- Boston mutters, "I don't want to sound stupid."
- Angeline and Kianna are giggling but not doing the task.

You pause and realize what's happening:

They understand the task. They know the vocabulary.

But they're uncomfortable using the language aloud.

This isn't a comprehension issue. It's a confidence-and-engagement issue.

You need a move that will lower the stakes and raise the energy without abandoning your learning goal.

How Might You Respond?

- What instructional and engagement moves could help students feel safe and willing to take risks with language?
- How can you increase participation without putting students on the spot?
- What structures or supports might boost confidence and bring fun back into speaking practice?

Chapter 6

Differentiation Moves

"I like how we get to pick different things to do. It's like a learning buffet!" —**Grade 3 student**

Walk into any classroom and you'll quickly see that no two students are the same. Each learner brings a unique mix of strengths, needs, interests, and experiences. That's both the beauty and the challenge of teaching.

This is where differentiation moves shine. These are the choices you make—before and during instruction—to ensure every student has access to meaningful learning. Differentiation isn't about designing twenty-five separate lesson plans. It's about using flexible, intentional strategies that help each student grow from where they are.

Differentiation moves keep the learning door open for everyone.

Why These Moves Matter

Differentiation moves aren't about lowering the bar. They're about lifting every learner to it. When you offer multiple ways for students to access content, engage with learning, and demonstrate understanding, you make learning possible for everyone.

Strong differentiation moves allow you to:

- Provide the right level of support and challenge for each learner.
- Increase access without lowering expectations.

- Help students feel successful, capable, and seen.
- Build equity into your everyday instruction.
- Encourage student agency and independence.

When learning fits the learner, confidence follows.

So, What Are Differentiation Moves?

Differentiation moves are instructional strategies that meet the wide range of learners in your classroom. Some are built into your planning, like offering tiered tasks or creating choice boards. Others happen in the moment, like adjusting questioning techniques or regrouping students to better match readiness levels.

Whether a student needs more support or an extra challenge, differentiation moves help you meet them where they are and move them forward. You don't need dozens of strategies—just a few strong tools and the willingness to adjust.

When Fast Isn't Fair

One of my favorite memories from elementary school was playing "Around the World." When my teacher pulled out those math flash cards, I was all in. I knew my multiplication facts well and could come up with the answers in an instant. It felt good to be faster than my peers and get to travel ***around the world*** in my classroom.

There was a common understanding in my class of who might win, who didn't have a chance, and where the competition really lay. There were only a few true contenders—and I was one of them.

Looking back now, I see this game for what it was. It wasn't about knowing multiplication facts; it was about who had quick processing speed.

I'm positive there were many kids in my class who also knew their facts but couldn't recall them as quickly. They needed more time to process and respond. For those students, I'm sure this game wasn't fun—and probably not something they remember as fondly as I once did.

As a teacher, I learned that students who need more time to process often compare themselves to their peers and eventually conclude that they're "stupid" because it takes them longer.

Stop and think about how often we—perhaps unknowingly—reward speed in our classrooms: students who raise their hand first often get called on, and those who finish tasks quickly get free time or less homework.

What messages are we giving to kids who are just as capable but need more time? How do we maintain their self-esteem by giving them opportunities to shine?

What Makes These Moves Work?

Differentiation moves are about recognizing each student's unique starting point and guiding them toward meaningful growth. At their heart, these strategies open the door to learning for everyone while maintaining high expectations and removing obstacles that might hold students back.

Here's what strong differentiation moves do:

Provide Equitable Access

You adapt how content is delivered so every student can engage fully without sacrificing rigor or depth.

Support Individual Growth

You meet students at their starting point, offering just-right challenges that build confidence and momentum.

Promote Motivation

When students see themselves in the work and believe they can succeed, they're more likely to stay invested and push through challenges.

Build Student Ownership

You give students meaningful choices and invite them to take the lead, developing independence and agency.

The most impactful differentiation strategies aren't about adding more work—they're about making smart choices. They share a few common qualities:

- **Student-Centered** – You start with your learners—their needs, strengths, and preferences—not just the curriculum.
- **Proactive** – You plan with a range of needs in mind, instead of scrambling to adjust after problems arise.
- **Flexible** – You pivot based on what you observe in real time, adjusting tasks, supports, or pacing as needed.
- **Data-Informed** – You use both formal and informal evidence to guide your decisions—assessments, exit tickets, conversations, observations, and student work.
- **Sustainable** – You embed differentiation into daily routines, so it becomes part of your teaching flow, not an exhausting add-on.

When your moves hit these marks, students feel supported without being singled out. They experience success without limits and begin to see themselves as capable, confident learners.

When every student can access the learning, every student can succeed.

Real Talk: What This Looks Like in Action

Let's say you're launching a writing assignment. You've explained the task. You can see some students are already diving in, but others are frozen.

What do you do?

- You offer three different writing prompts—***choice board move.***
- You pair students to brainstorm ideas—***peer support move.***
- You circulate and offer sentence stems or guiding questions—***scaffolded questioning move.***
- You check in with a few students and adjust the deadline for those who need more time—***flexibility move.***
- You let one confident student serve as a writing coach—***student expert move.***

That's not five different lesson plans. That's one differentiated approach that supports *everyone* in getting started—and getting somewhere.

You Don't Have to Do It All at Once

If "tailoring every lesson for every student" sounds overwhelming, remember that differentiation means working smarter, not harder.

Start small:

- Offer one flexible grouping opportunity each week.
- Give two options for how students can show their learning.
- Use data to adjust one part of tomorrow's lesson.
- Add one scaffolded question to your next discussion.

Small shifts lead to big impact.

Let's Explore: 16 Differentiation Moves

On the following pages, we'll explore sixteen teacher moves that help you reach more learners, promote equity, and personalize learning—without burning out:

Timely Feedback
Small Group Instruction
Scaffolded Writing Prompts
Parallel Tasks
Tiered Tasks
Curriculum Compacting
Flexible Grouping
Learning Stations
Choice Boards
Learning Menus
Student Experts
Checklists
Differentiated Rubrics
Multiple Means of Assessment
Enrichment Opportunities
Goal Setting

Let's take a closer look at each.

Timely Feedback

Purpose:

To provide immediate, student-specific guidance that helps correct errors, reinforce effective strategies, and maintain motivation.

Description:

This strategy involves using feedback as a tool for growth, not just evaluation. When you respond quickly and clearly, students understand what they're doing well and what they can do next. This builds confidence, sharpens skills, and makes learning more efficient. By offering feedback in the moment, you keep learning on track and prevent misunderstandings from becoming habits.

How to Use It:

1. Address Missteps Promptly

Step in as soon as you notice an error so students can adjust before moving on.

2. Reinforce Positive Practices

Highlight what students are doing correctly to build confidence and encourage them to repeat strong strategies. For example:

- "You stopped to reread when something didn't make sense—that's exactly what good readers do."
- "Your opening sentence grabs attention right away. Use that same strong voice in the rest of your paragraph."

3. Be Specific and Actionable

Give clear, direct feedback students can act on right away. Focus on both strengths and next steps. For example:

- "You labeled your diagram correctly. Now add units to your measurements so it's more precise."
- "You set up the equation correctly—that's a strong start. Now check your multiplication in step three to make sure your answer is accurate."

4. Keep the Flow

Offer feedback naturally within the learning process, without disrupting momentum.

Example: During a geometry lesson, a student labels a square as a rectangle. You say, "You're right that a square has four sides and four right angles—that's just like a rectangle. But remember, a square is a special kind of rectangle because all its sides are the same length. Let's double-check your labels together."

When to Use It:

- During guided practice and independent work
- While circulating in group discussions or projects
- Anytime students are applying new learning and need support in real time

Why It Works:

✓ Prevents errors from becoming ingrained
✓ Builds confidence through immediate reinforcement
✓ Keeps learning active and responsive
✓ Guides students toward independence and mastery

Small Group Instruction

Purpose:

To provide focused, targeted instruction that matches students' readiness levels, interests, or learning needs.

Description:

This strategy involves teaching in small groups to deliver just-right instruction while the rest of the class works independently or collaboratively. Groups are flexible and shift as student needs change, ensuring everyone can access the core learning goals. By working in smaller groups, you can personalize support, challenge advanced learners, and keep all students engaged in meaningful practice.

How to Use It:

1. **Clarify the Learning Goal**

   Identify the core concept or skill all students need to develop.

2. **Form Flexible Groups**

   Group students based on current understanding, interests, or learning profiles. Keep groups dynamic and fluid.

3. **Plan Differentiated Tasks**

   Prepare materials that meet each group's needs—such as scaffolds for struggling learners, practice for on-level learners, or enrichment tasks for advanced learners.

4. **Rotate and Support**

   Meet with one group at a time to provide guided instruction, feedback, or practice. Meanwhile, other students engage in meaningful independent tasks, centers, or collaborative work.

5. **Monitor Progress**

   Use questioning, observation, or quick checks to track growth and regroup students as needed.

Example: After a whole-class mini-lesson on making inferences, you use a short reading passage and a few comprehension questions to check student understanding. Based on their responses, you form three small groups: one group works with you on identifying key details in the text because they need more support with basic comprehension, another group practices making simple inferences with sentence starters, and a third group extends the skill by comparing two texts and discussing deeper themes. As students demonstrate progress, you regroup them to match their current needs.

When to Use It:

- When students need varying levels of support to master the same skill
- With content-area lessons where skills can be differentiated
- During guided reading or writer's workshop

Why It Works:

✓ Provides targeted, student-centered instruction

✓ Builds confidence and independence

✓ Increases engagement by matching tasks to readiness levels

✓ Creates space for stronger teacher-student connections

Scaffolded Writing Prompts

Purpose:

To support all learners by offering writing tasks at varying levels of complexity, ensuring access to content while encouraging higher-order thinking.

Description:

This strategy involves providing tiered writing prompts that allow students to respond at their own level of readiness. Struggling learners can engage meaningfully, while advanced learners are challenged to extend their ideas. By scaffolding prompts, you promote equity, growth, and critical thinking in writing tasks.

How to Use It:

1. **Design Tiered Prompts**

   Create prompts that progress from recall to analysis and creation, so students can enter at an accessible level and move toward deeper thinking.

2. **Offer Choice or Assign Levels**

   Let students select a prompt that fits their readiness, or assign prompts based on observation, assessment, or learning goals.

3. **Encourage Growth**

   Guide students to build on their responses. For example, after completing a recall-level prompt, encourage them to try an explanatory or creative one.

Example: In a social studies lesson, you provide scaffolded writing prompts after reading about early explorers:

- **Recall:** List three facts you learned about the explorers.
- **Explain:** Explain why the explorers decided to take the risk of traveling into unknown lands.
- **Apply:** How do you think these historical explorations are similar to or different from modern space exploration?
- **Create:** Imagine you are an explorer today. Write a journal entry about your first day in a new land.

When to Use It:

- During independent practice or journal writing
- For reading responses or exit tickets
- To differentiate writing tasks in any subject area
- When you want students to practice critical thinking and creativity through writing

Why It Works:

✓ Meets students where they are with accessible entry points
✓ Encourages growth by scaffolding toward more complex thinking
✓ Promotes inclusion and differentiation in writing tasks
✓ Builds confidence by valuing all levels of student response

Parallel Tasks

Purpose:

To provide students with different pathways to practice the same core concept, ensuring each learner is challenged appropriately while working toward the same goal.

Description:

This strategy involves designing multiple versions of a task at varying levels of complexity, all focused on the same big idea. Parallel tasks ensure equitable access, appropriate challenge, and shared learning goals.

How to Use It:

1. Identify the Core Concept

Pinpoint the essential skill or learning outcome that all students need to understand.

2. Design Parallel Tasks

Adjust the process, materials, level of abstraction, or supports provided, while keeping the learning goal consistent.

3. Differentiate the Approach

Parallel tasks might vary in:

- Complexity (simple to advanced)
- Level of scaffolds (visuals, manipulatives, or contextual supports)
- Number of steps or degree of independence required

4. Assign or Offer Choice

Place students into tasks based on readiness (using observation or assessment) or let them choose, with your guidance, to ensure the challenge is appropriate.

Example: During a lesson on summarizing nonfiction, all students are asked to write a summary, but the articles vary in complexity. One group reads a shorter article about animal habitats written at a lower reading level, while another group reads a longer, more complex article about climate change and its effects on habitats. Each group writes a summary of their article, ensuring all students practice the same core skill of summarizing while working at their readiness level.

When to Use It:

- When students show varied readiness levels for the same concept
- During math problem-solving or science investigations
- In literacy tasks that can be modified by complexity or support
- In cross-curricular projects where equitable access is essential

Why It Works:

- ✓ Promotes equity by meeting students at their level
- ✓ Ensures all learners engage with the same big idea
- ✓ Encourages growth by providing just-right challenges
- ✓ Builds confidence while maintaining academic rigor

Tiered Tasks

Purpose:

To give all students meaningful access to the same core concept by designing assignments at different levels of complexity to ensure every learner is appropriately challenged.

Description:

This strategy involves creating multiple entry points into the same learning goal. Each task targets the same big idea but varies in depth, process, or product. By tiering tasks, you help students build confidence, stretch their thinking, and succeed while still being held to rigorous expectations.

How to Use It:

1. **Clarify the Learning Goal**

   Identify the essential skill or concept all students will work toward.

2. **Design Tiered Learning Tasks**

   Create multiple tasks of different complexity, all aligned to the same objective. Adjust the amount of scaffolding, the depth of analysis, or the type of product students create.

3. **Group or Assign Based on Readiness**

   Use observations, prior work, or conferencing to guide students to the task that best matches their needs. Encourage growth by challenging them at the edge of their comfort zone.

4. **Provide Clear Instructions and Supports**

   Offer checklists, models, or rubrics so students know what success looks like at each level.

5. **Encourage Movement and Growth**

   Allow students to progress to more complex tasks as they build skills and confidence.

Example: For a science unit on the needs of living things, tasks may include:

- **Tier 1 (Foundational):** Matching pictures of animals with food, water, shelter, and air.
- **Tier 2 (Grade Level):** Drawing and labeling a habitat for an animal of choice, showing how it meets its needs. Then, writing 1–2 sentences explaining the drawing.
- **Tier 3 (Extension):** Creating a mini book describing the needs of different animals in various environments (forest, ocean, desert), including labeled diagrams and written explanations.

When to Use It:

- During guided practice when readiness levels vary
- In science, literacy, or math tasks that can be scaled by complexity
- For project-based learning or skill-building activities
- Anytime you want to promote equity while keeping expectations high

Why It Works:

✓ Provides multiple entry points into the same concept

✓ Promotes equity by meeting students at their level

✓ Encourages growth without lowering expectations

✓ Builds confidence and engagement for all learners

Curriculum Compacting

Purpose:

To prevent advanced learners from repeating content they've already mastered by providing opportunities for enrichment and deeper exploration.

Description:

This strategy involves streamlining instruction by assessing what students already know, removing unnecessary review, and replacing it with meaningful, challenging learning experiences. This approach keeps students engaged, promotes higher-order thinking, and ensures that instructional time is used effectively for all learners.

How to Use It:

1. Assess Prior Knowledge

Use pre-assessments, quick checks, or student work samples to identify mastered skills or concepts.

2. Eliminate Redundant Practice

Remove tasks or assignments that cover content students have already demonstrated mastery in.

3. Provide Enrichment Opportunities

Replace skipped tasks with activities that extend learning, such as independent research, creative projects, or real-world problem-solving.

4. Monitor Progress

Check in regularly to ensure enrichment tasks remain challenging, engaging, and connected to learning goals.

Example: In a social studies unit on government, you give a quick pre-assessment. Students who show mastery of the three levels of government skip the review lessons and instead research a real-world civic issue in their community. They create a proposal for how the local government could address it, present their ideas to the class, and reflect on how local decision-making impacts citizens.

When to Use It:

- When students consistently show mastery before or during a unit
- In subjects with repetitive practice (e.g., math facts, spelling, grammar)
- When students are already fluent in core concepts

Why It Works:

✓ Keeps advanced learners challenged and motivated

✓ Maximizes instructional time by eliminating redundancy

✓ Promotes deeper, real-world learning experiences

✓ Supports equity by ensuring all students are appropriately challenged

Flexible Grouping

Purpose:

To maximize learning by grouping students in different ways based on the task, learning goal, or current needs.

Description:

This strategy involves intentionally shifting how students work together—sometimes by skill, sometimes by interest, and sometimes randomly. By using a fluid approach, you ensure that all students have opportunities to collaborate, take on new roles, and learn from diverse peers. Changing groups regularly supports both academic growth and social development while keeping classroom dynamics fresh and engaging.

How to Use It:

1. Create Groups Based on Purpose

Form groups that match the learning goal. Examples include:

- By skill level—for targeted instruction or guided practice
- By interest or choice—for project-based learning or passion projects
- By random selection—to promote teamwork and build classroom community

2. Use a Variety of Formats

Rotate between pairs, triads, small groups, or larger collaborative teams depending on the task.

3. Shift Groups Regularly

Reorganize groups often so students work with different classmates, try new roles, and practice multiple skills.

4. Monitor and Support

Circulate to observe group interactions, offer scaffolding, and adjust as needed so all students remain engaged and productive.

Example: During a math lesson on measurement, you organize three flexible groups. One group measures classroom objects using nonstandard units like paperclips or linking cubes. Another group practices measuring with rulers in centimeters, comparing which objects are longer or shorter. A third group works on a challenge task—measuring the length of the classroom carpet and estimating how many desks could fit along one side. You rotate the groups, so every student experiences hands-on practice and new challenges.

When to Use It:

- During cooperative learning activities
- In station or center rotations
- For project-based or inquiry learning
- During small group instruction across subjects

Why It Works:

- ✓ Provides multiple pathways for differentiation
- ✓ Builds collaboration and communication skills
- ✓ Keeps classroom dynamics fresh and engaging
- ✓ Helps students learn from peers with diverse strengths

Learning Stations

Purpose:

To give students multiple opportunities to practice, explore, and extend learning through varied, interactive tasks.

Description:

This strategy involves setting up small group or independent activity centers around the classroom that offer tasks at different levels of complexity, use varied modalities, and give students choice. Stations help students take ownership of their learning while giving you time to work with individuals or small groups.

How to Use It:

1. Set Clear Objectives

Identify the skills or concepts you want students to strengthen or extend.

2. Design the Stations

Create a range of activities that include varied learning styles—hands-on, collaborative, independent, or digital.

3. Prepare Materials and Directions

Provide clear written or visual instructions at each station, along with necessary materials. Use timers or posted rotations for smooth movement.

4. Teach the Routine

Model how students should rotate, manage materials, and stay on task. Practice the procedure until it runs smoothly.

5. Build in Accountability

Use recording sheets, math journals, or reflection tasks so students track their own work and you gather evidence of learning.

Example: Your class is reviewing fractions. You set up four stations:

- **Station 1:** Sort fraction cards by matching visual models, numbers, and words.
- **Station 2:** Solve real-life word problems involving recipes, shopping, or measurement.
- **Station 3:** Play a board game where students add, subtract, or compare fractions.
- **Station 4:** Use an online platform for fraction practice with immediate feedback.

Students rotate in small groups, giving them access to varied practice, peer collaboration, and targeted teacher check-ins.

When to Use It:

- During guided practice while you meet with small groups
- When reviewing or reinforcing previously taught skills
- For differentiating practice and offering choice
- To introduce new concepts in an interactive, exploratory way

Why It Works:

✓ Increases engagement and active participation

✓ Provides differentiated pathways for practice and extension

✓ Builds independence and accountability

Choice Boards

Purpose:

To give students voice and choice in how they demonstrate learning, increasing engagement while ensuring everyone works toward the same academic goal.

Description:

This strategy involves providing task options—usually arranged in a grid—that allow students to select how they will practice or show understanding of a concept. By offering multiple pathways, choice boards make learning more personalized, engaging, and inclusive of different interests and strengths.

How to Use It:

1. Design the Board

Create a 3x3 or 4x4 grid with varied task options. Include different products, processes, and approaches to learning.

2. Align Tasks to the Learning Goal

Ensure all choices connect to the same learning objective so that no matter what task students pick, they meet curriculum expectations.

3. Offer Variety

Include options that appeal to different learning preferences—visual, kinesthetic, written, digital, or collaborative.

4. Provide Clear Criteria

Use rubrics, checklists, or exemplars so students understand expectations for success across all choices.

5. Encourage Student Ownership

Allow students to select one or more activities from the board. This fosters autonomy, motivation, and pride in their work.

Example: After a unit on natural disasters and their impact on communities, you provide a **Geography Choice Board** with options to demonstrate understanding of the same big idea: how geography influences disaster preparedness.

Choice Board Options:

- Write a news article describing how a recent natural disaster affected a region and why geography played a role in its severity.
- Design a disaster preparedness plan for a community near a fault line, volcano, or floodplain.
- Build a 3D model (digital or physical) of a city showing how geography shapes risk zones and evacuation routes.
- Record a public service announcement encouraging disaster readiness, explaining how local geography impacts planning.
- Use a digital mapping tool to compare two regions impacted by different disasters, annotating geographic factors.
- Write and perform a mock interview between a geographer and a government official about disaster mitigation.

When to Use It:

- During assessments to allow multiple ways of showing mastery
- In project-based learning to give students flexibility and creativity
- When differentiating by readiness, interest, or learning style
- Anytime you want to increase engagement through personalized learning

Why It Works:

✓ Provides students with ownership of their learning

✓ Ensures equity by aligning all tasks to the same learning goal

✓ Builds motivation by tapping into interests and strengths

✓ Supports differentiation without creating separate lessons

Learning Menus

Purpose:

To offer students structured choices for engaging with content and demonstrating understanding while ensuring essential learning goals are met.

Description:

This strategy involves creating a framework of tasks organized like a restaurant menu—appetizers, main courses, and desserts—that provide variety and differentiation. This structure fosters autonomy, creativity, and ownership while keeping learning rigorous and goal focused.

How to Use It:

1. Design the Menu

Create a menu that includes a variety of task options. A common structure is:

- **Appetizers:** Warm-up tasks or foundational skill practice.
- **Main Courses:** Core assignments all students must complete, aligned with the learning goals.
- **Desserts:** Optional enrichment or challenge activities for early finishers or advanced learners

2. Differentiate the Tasks

Include activities that vary in complexity and learning style—writing, visuals, technology, collaboration, or independent work.

3. Set Clear Expectations

Provide clear guidelines, success criteria, and timelines for each option. Use rubrics or checklists to help students track their progress.

4. Allow Student Choice

Give students flexibility to select appetizer and dessert options, while ensuring all complete the main course.

Example: In a geography class on landforms, you provide this **Learning Menu:**

- *Appetizer (Choose One):*
  - » Define key vocabulary terms related to landforms.
  - » Label a blank map with different types of landforms.
- *Main Course (Complete Both):*
  - » Write a paragraph explaining how mountains, valleys, and plateaus are formed.
  - » Create a diagram or digital drawing showing examples of landforms in your region.
- *Dessert (Optional):*
  - » Research a famous landform and create a virtual tour using slides or a digital app.
  - » Write a fictional travel journal describing a visit to three different landforms.

When to Use It:

- During project-based learning
- As review or practice after a unit
- During assessments to allow multiple ways of showing mastery

Why It Works:

✓ Increases engagement by offering variety and choice

✓ Supports differentiation across readiness levels, interests, and learning styles

✓ Promotes autonomy and responsibility for learning

✓ Ensures all students master essential content

Student Experts

Purpose:

To empower students who have mastered a concept or skill to support their peers, reinforcing their own learning while fostering collaboration and leadership in the classroom.

Description:

This strategy involves inviting students who have mastered a concept or skill to act as "experts" and support their peers. By sharing knowledge with classmates, student experts reinforce their own learning, build confidence, and foster collaboration. This approach adds layers of scaffolding and helps create a classroom culture where students learn with and from one another.

How to Use It:

1. Identify Expertise

Observe strengths during lessons or use assessments to determine which students have mastered specific skills or concepts.

2. Assign Roles Purposefully

Invite student experts to circulate during work time, lead small demonstrations, or clarify steps for peers. Make the role voluntary and position it as an opportunity, not extra work.

3. Coach on Peer Support

Teach student experts how to guide learning—asking questions, modeling strategies, and prompting peers—without simply giving answers.

4. Balance the Dynamic

Reinforce that experts are helpers, not authority figures. Ensure all students feel valued, whether they are providing or receiving support.

5. Rotate Opportunities

Offer different students the chance to act as experts over time in various subjects or tasks, building leadership and shared responsibility.

Example: In music class, you notice a few students are confident with playing simple melodies on the recorder. You invite them to act as "music coaches" during practice time. They circulate, demonstrate finger placement, and offer tips to classmates who are still learning. As they teach, their own skills strengthen while their peers gain extra support.

When to Use It:

- During guided or independent practice
- In small group stations
- During review or reteaching sessions
- In project-based learning where diverse skills are needed

Why It Works:

✓ Reinforces learning through teaching

✓ Promotes student leadership and confidence

✓ Builds a collaborative classroom culture

✓ Provides peer-to-peer scaffolding that lightens teacher workload

Checklists

Purpose:

To provide students with a clear, step-by-step guide for completing tasks, while promoting independence, organization, and accountability.

Description:

This strategy involves giving students a checklist that breaks a task into clear, manageable steps. By tracking their progress and checking off items as they go, students build independence, stay organized, and hold themselves accountable. Checklists reduce overwhelm, clarify expectations, and help learners develop planning and self-monitoring skills they can use across subjects.

How to Use It:

1. **Break Down the Task**

   List the key steps or components in clear, simple language so students know exactly what needs to be done.

2. **Model Its Use**

   Show students how to check off items as they complete them and demonstrate how to use the list to stay organized.

3. **Differentiate the Format**

   Provide visual checklists with icons or pictures for younger learners or those needing extra support. Older students can use digital or self-created checklists.

4. **Encourage Independence**

   Build routines where students use checklists to manage daily work, long-term projects, or classroom jobs without relying solely on teacher reminders.

5. **Reflect on Progress**

   At the end of the task, have students review the checklist to self-assess their effort and completeness.

Example: During writer's workshop, you give students a **Paragraph Checklist** that includes:

- I wrote a topic sentence.
- I included at least three details.
- I used transition words.
- I wrote a closing sentence.
- I checked my spelling and punctuation.

You encourage students to use the checklist during drafting and again before turning in their work, helping them self-assess and strengthen their writing.

When to Use It:

- During writing tasks to guide structure and revision
- For multi-step projects or experiments
- As part of classroom routines (e.g., packing up, cleaning, organizing)
- To build independence in time management and task completion

Why It Works:

✓ Makes expectations clear and concrete
✓ Promotes independence and self-monitoring
✓ Reduces overwhelm by breaking tasks into steps
✓ Helps students develop organizational skills

Differentiated Rubrics

Purpose:

To provide students with clear success criteria for a task, helping them understand expectations, monitor progress, and strive for higher levels of quality in their work.

Description:

This strategy involves outlining the success criteria and performance levels for the core rubric. Then modifying it for both emerging and advanced learners. Rubrics promote fairness, transparency, and self-reflection, while encouraging students to take ownership of the learning process.

How to Use It:

1. **Define Clear Criteria**

   Identify the key skills or elements students need to demonstrate (e.g., accuracy, organization, creativity, communication).

2. **Create Performance Levels**

   Write descriptors that show what the skill looks like at different levels of quality. Use student-friendly language and concrete examples, and prepare modified versions for emerging and advanced learners.

3. **Introduce and Model**

   Walk students through the rubric before they begin. Model how to interpret each level and what it looks like in practice.

4. **Use During the Process**

   Encourage students to check their work against the rubric as they draft, revise, or practice.

5. **Reflect and Revise**

   Have students use the rubric for self- or peer-assessment, then adjust their work before submitting.

Example: For a social studies presentation, you provide students with differentiated rubrics:

- **Core Rubric**
- **Supported Version (for emerging learners)**
    - » Uses simple language with visuals (e.g., smiley faces, thumbs up/down icons).
    - » Provides concrete examples of what each criterion looks like in practice.
- **Extended Version (for advanced learners)**
    - » Adds criteria for persuasive language, audience engagement, and answering follow-up questions.

You guide students to use the rubric before, during, and after their project to prepare, self-reflect, and improve their performance.

When to Use It:

- During projects, presentations, or performances
- For writing tasks that require multiple drafts and revisions
- For summative assessments

Why It Works:

✓ Makes expectations transparent and consistent

✓ Guides students toward higher-quality work

✓ Encourages self- and peer-assessment

✓ Supports growth by showing what improvement looks like

Multiple Means of Assessment

Purpose:

To give all students equitable opportunities to demonstrate their learning by offering a variety of assessment formats that match their strengths, interests, and needs.

Description:

This strategy involves offering students multiple ways—such as written, oral, visual, or hands-on demonstrations—to show their learning. By giving options, you honor student voice, support accessibility, and ensure every learner can demonstrate understanding in meaningful ways.

How to Use It:

1. **Clarify the Learning Goal**

   Identify the essential knowledge or skill that all students must demonstrate, regardless of the assessment format.

2. **Offer a Range of Options**

   Design assessments in varied formats (e.g., reports, presentations, models, videos, artwork). Ensure each option measures the same outcome.

3. **Provide Clear Success Criteria**

   Establish consistent expectations across all formats.

4. **Support Student Choice**

   Allow students to select the method that best suits their learning style, or assign based on readiness and accessibility needs.

5. **Reflect and Adjust**

   Use assessment results to guide instruction, celebrate diverse strengths, and identify areas for growth.

Example: In a science unit on electricity, you ask students to demonstrate their understanding of how circuits work. They can choose to:

- **Write:** a detailed report explaining the function and flow of a circuit
- **Build:** a simple working circuit model and present it to the class
- **Record:** a video tutorial using props for younger students
- **Design:** an infographic or poster illustrating the parts of a circuit and how they work

All options address the same learning outcome but provide flexible ways for students to express their knowledge.

When to Use It:

- For summative assessments
- For unit reviews or culminating activities
- In project-based learning

Why It Works:

✓ Promotes equity and inclusion
✓ Encourages creativity and ownership of learning
✓ Provides a fuller picture of student understanding
✓ Maintains rigor while allowing choice

Enrichment Opportunities

Purpose:

To challenge advanced learners by extending their learning beyond grade-level expectations, promoting deeper understanding, critical thinking, and creativity.

Description:

This strategy involves designing opportunities for students who have already mastered core skills or concepts to explore advanced tasks, independent projects, and real-world applications. By engaging in higher-level work, students spark curiosity, deepen understanding, and build new skills.

How to Use It:

1. **Assess Prior Knowledge**

   Use pre-assessments, checklists, or observations to determine which students have already mastered the content.

2. **Compact the Curriculum**

   Let proficient students skip repetitive practice or review activities so they can move on to enrichment.

3. **Design Enrichment Activities**

   Provide challenging options such as open-ended projects, real-world problem-solving, independent research, or creative applications.

4. **Set Clear Goals and Expectations**

   Explain how enrichment tasks align with learning goals and establish criteria for success.

5. **Monitor and Support**

   Check in regularly, provide feedback, and offer resources to keep students motivated and progressing.

6. **Celebrate Achievement**

   Showcase student work to validate their efforts and inspire ongoing curiosity.

Example: During language arts class, you notice that some students score high on a comprehension pre-assessment. Instead of giving them standard practice questions, you let them select a novel of their choice and create a literary magazine. Their magazine might include a character interview, a comic strip of a key scene, and an opinion article debating a theme. This project encourages creativity, deeper analysis, and advanced writing skills.

When to Use It:

- When students consistently perform above grade level in specific subjects or skills
- During reading, math, science, or social studies units with clear mastery points
- To promote independent inquiry, problem-solving, or project-based learning
- To keep advanced learners challenged and engaged while others build foundational skills

Why It Works:

✓ Prevents boredom by eliminating redundant work

✓ Challenges students at their readiness level

✓ Promotes higher-order thinking and creativity

✓ Validates student strengths and fosters motivation

Goal Setting

Purpose:

To empower students to take ownership of their learning by identifying meaningful objectives, tracking progress, and celebrating growth.

Description:

This strategy involves guiding students to set specific, realistic goals that break big challenges into manageable steps. Goal setting helps students build motivation, develop self-awareness, and monitor improvement, fostering accountability and a growth mindset.

How to Use It:

1. Meet Individually

Hold brief student conferences to identify strengths, challenges, and areas for growth. Focus on goals that are relevant and attainable.

2. Set Clear Goals

Guide students in writing SMART goals—Specific, Measurable, Achievable, Relevant, and Time-bound.

3. Create Visual Trackers

Use bar graphs, progress charts, sticker charts, or checklists to make growth visible and motivating.

4. Monitor and Reflect

Schedule regular check-ins to review progress, adjust goals if needed, and celebrate achievements. Encourage reflection on which strategies are helping.

Example: During math class, you help a student working on multiplication fluency set a goal: "I will correctly complete twenty multiplication problems in under five minutes by the end of the month." The student tracks progress on a personal graph each week and reflects on strategies like skip-counting or using flashcards.

When to Use It:

- At the start of a new unit or skill cycle
- As part of progress monitoring or report card reflections
- During student-led conferences

Why It Works:

✓ Builds student motivation through personalized goals

✓ Fosters self-awareness and metacognition

✓ Makes growth visible and concrete

✓ Encourages perseverance and a growth mindset

Final Thoughts

Differentiation isn't about doing more—it's about doing what matters. At its core, it's a mindset: a commitment to seeing each student as an individual with unique strengths, needs, and potential. When you use differentiation moves with intention, you create a classroom where *every* learner feels seen, supported, and capable of success.

It doesn't have to be complicated. You don't need to write twenty-five different lesson plans. You're making smart, flexible adjustments that help students access the content, engage meaningfully, and grow from wherever they're starting.

Over time, small, intentional shifts build something powerful: a classroom culture rooted in equity, respect, and growth. Students gain confidence. They take ownership. They begin to believe, "I *can* do this."

So, take it one move at a time. Stay curious, stay responsive, and keep refining your practice. When you differentiate with purpose, you're not just teaching content—you're developing confident, capable learners ready for whatever comes next.

Up Next

While differentiation is about designing learning to meet students where they are, adaptive moves are about responding in the moment—pivoting your instruction when a lesson takes an unexpected turn, a misconception surfaces, or the class energy shifts.

In the next chapter, we'll explore adaptive moves: how to adjust on the fly so every student stays engaged and supported, no matter what the day brings.

PUTTING IT INTO PRACTICE

Now that you've seen the why and how behind effective differentiation moves, let's explore what they might look like in real life.

The following scenarios are pulled from common classroom moments—ones that every teacher has faced in some form. Each one invites you to pause, reflect, and consider:

What moves might I make in this moment?

This is where theory meets practice—and where your instincts and toolkit come together.

SCENARIOS

The Constant Disrupter

The Juggling Act

One Lesson, Many Needs

Scenario 1: The Constant Disrupter

It's mid-morning in your grade 3 classroom, and students are working on a writing assignment about their favorite place. Most are quietly brainstorming or drafting in their notebooks.

Except for Ethan.

Ethan has barely written a word. Instead, he's:

- Rolling his pencil off the desk and diving under the table to get it.
- Reaching across to poke Leila's elbow every few minutes.
- Whispering to Jaxon about Minecraft while Jaxon tries to focus.
- Walking over to the window to look outside, then tapping the glass with both hands.

You've already redirected him twice—gently and firmly.

You've offered a fidget, a movement break, and a visual prompt.

Still, Ethan struggles to focus for more than a few seconds, and his behavior is pulling others off-task too.

Leila finally turns to you and says in a whisper, "Can you make him stop?"

Jaxon groans and moves to the other side of the room.

You can feel the patience in the room thinning.

Ethan doesn't seem to notice—or maybe he notices *everything* at once.

You pause. You know this isn't defiance. It's a student who *wants* to do well...but can't yet regulate on his own.

How Might You Respond?

- How can you support Ethan's need for movement, attention, and connection while also protecting the learning environment?
- What proactive teacher moves might help him stay regulated and focused without constant redirection?
- How do you build a plan that helps Ethan *and* his peers feel supported?

Scenario 2: The Juggling Act

It's the start of your guided reading block in your grade 1 classroom. You've set up three small groups with leveled texts and a few independent literacy stations: read-to-self, word work, and listening center.

Your goal is to work with your early readers on decoding strategies.

But as you begin with your group, it quickly becomes clear that things aren't running as smoothly as planned.

- Jayden is reading well above grade level and is flying through the books. He's finished two already and is now distracting a nearby group.
- Olivia is still learning letter-sound correspondence. She sits frozen at the word work station, unsure of what to do, even though you've modeled it before.
- Tariq and Sophie, both emerging readers, are paired together for partner reading. Tariq does all the reading while Sophie barely looks at the page.
- Meanwhile, Lily, who has an IEP for speech and language, is quietly trying to read aloud to herself—but the background noise is overwhelming her.
- Your own guided group is distracted, and you've repeated the same sentence three times while redirecting behaviors around the room.

You take a deep breath. You know they all need something different...yet somehow, they all need it at the same time.

How Might You Respond?

- What differentiation moves could help you meet these varied reading needs without overcomplicating your routine?
- How might you provide appropriate challenge, support, and structure to keep all students engaged?
- What tools or routines could help make this block more manageable and effective?

Scenario 3: One Lesson, Many Needs

It's late morning in your grade 4 classroom, and you're launching a lesson on multi-digit multiplication. You've planned carefully. Your mini lesson includes visual modeling, worked examples, and a guided practice task that students will complete in pairs.

But as soon as students begin working, the cracks start to show.

- Eli, who has a learning disability in math, immediately shuts down. He stares at the blank page and says, "This is too hard. I don't get any of it."
- Layla, who is on an IEP for ADHD, bounces between desks, asking everyone for help without waiting for an answer.
- Ava, your gifted student, finishes all four problems in record time and looks around bored.
- Noah raises his hand and says loudly, "Why do we have to do this again? We just did this yesterday."
- Two ELL students in the back look confused. They're quietly whispering in their home language, trying to make sense of the instructions.
- Meanwhile, the rest of the class is buzzing with low-level confusion, and several students are calling your name at once.

You suddenly feel like you're teaching six different grades at the same time.

You've differentiated in your planning... but now you're in the moment. And the moment is messy.

How Might You Respond?

- What real-time differentiation moves can you make to support students at very different readiness levels?
- How can you provide scaffolding without slowing down the whole class or leaving advanced learners bored?
- What tools, routines, or grouping strategies could help you manage these needs without burning out?

Chapter 7

Adaptive Moves

"We were supposed to do a test, but everyone was stressed. So, my teacher turned it into a review game." **—Grade 7 student**

Even the most thoughtful, well-prepared lesson can take an unexpected turn. Students get stuck. Energy fades. Disruptions appear out of nowhere. And sometimes, a strategy that soared yesterday just doesn't land today.

That's where adaptive moves come in—those quick, in-the-moment shifts that keep learning moving forward. Whether it's changing your pacing, offering another explanation, or swapping out an activity midstream, adaptive moves are about staying responsive to what's happening right now.

You don't need perfection. You need presence, awareness, and the willingness to pivot when the moment calls for it.

Adaptability turns challenges into opportunities for learning.

Why These Moves Matter

No two classes are identical, and no lesson ever unfolds exactly as imagined. Adaptive moves help you respond in real time, so learning doesn't stall when the unexpected happens.

With strong adaptive moves, you can:

- Keep students engaged and supported, even when plans shift.
- Address confusion or behavior issues before they derail learning.
- Make the most of every instructional minute.

- Model flexibility and problem-solving for your students.
- Foster a sense of safety, connection, and understanding.

When you pivot with purpose, you keep learning in motion.

So, What Are Adaptive Moves?

Adaptive moves are in-the-moment decisions you make during teaching to meet students where they are. They're not about scrapping your whole plan. They're about knowing when to stick with it and when to shift.

Sometimes that means slowing down when students look confused. Other times, it means changing your groupings, asking a different question, or weaving student interests into the conversation to re-engage attention.

Think of adaptive moves as your teaching "GPS"—constantly rerouting based on where your students **are**, not where you expected them to be.

Degrees of Learning

I grew up in Windsor, a city that borders Detroit. Every evening my parents watched a Detroit news station on television. Driving in our car, we listened to Detroit radio stations. It wasn't until I was well into my teens that I realized there were Canadian news and radio stations. I simply hadn't been exposed to them as a child.

Fast forward to my first student teaching placement. I had spent the entire weekend preparing to teach my first math lesson—temperature to grade 2 students.

I created a huge thermometer out of Bristol board so the students could help me manipulate it. I had prepared my lesson, and though I was filled with nervous anticipation, I felt ready.

As I began introducing the topic, I started with a conversation about the weather. I asked the students what they might wear in each season and used this prior knowledge to introduce the concept of temperature.

Using my Bristol board thermometer, I demonstrated how it worked, and we practiced setting temperatures for each season. "What season would it be if the thermometer read 90 degrees Fahrenheit?" I asked. Students quickly raised their hands to offer answers.

At the same time, my associate teacher quietly called my name. When I looked over, she motioned for me to come closer and gently reminded me that in Canada, we measure temperature in degrees Celsius.

My heart sank as my mind scrambled for what to do next.

What Makes These Moves Work?

At their core, adaptive moves are about being responsive and student-centered in the moment. They allow you to:

Overcome Learning Barriers

Step in quickly when students struggle, adjusting your approach without lowering expectations.

Enhance Engagement

Switch formats, add a quick collaborative moment, or connect the content to student interests when energy dips.

Address Challenges in Real Time

Handle confusion or disruptions calmly so you can keep instruction moving.

Maximize Teachable Moments

Pause the plan when curiosity or deeper understanding emerges, letting authentic learning take the lead.

Model Adaptability

Show students that flexibility and calm problem-solving are part of real-world success.

The most impactful adaptive moves share these qualities:

- **Flexible** – Willing to pivot based on what's happening now, not just the original plan.
- **Observant** – Attuned to body language, tone, and engagement levels—not just raised hands.
- **Proactive** – Prepared with backup options so you can respond with confidence.
- **Inclusive** – Adjustments benefit all learners, not just the loudest or fastest.
- **Calm** – Changes flow naturally, modeling composure for students.
- **Data-Informed** – Decisions are guided by student work, discussions, and check-ins.

When you adapt with intention, you don't just rescue lessons—you elevate them.

Adaptive moves allow you to teach with responsiveness, authenticity, and care, showing students that learning isn't about perfection—it's about progress, persistence, and openness to change.

Your calm response is the anchor in a shifting classroom.

Real Talk: What This Looks Like in Action

You're teaching a reading comprehension lesson. Midway through, you notice several students are stuck on unfamiliar vocabulary, and frustration is building.

What do you do?

- ◆ You pause to model a think-aloud of how to use context clues—*scaffolding move.*
- ◆ You pair students to discuss and decode words together—*collaborative support move.*
- ◆ You swap the dense text for a shorter passage on the same skill—*flexible resource move.*

None of that was in the plan. But it keeps students engaged, supported, and moving forward.

That's the power of adaptive teaching.

You Don't Have to It All at Once

Adaptive teaching isn't about reacting perfectly. It's about staying tuned in and choosing your next best move.

Start simple:

- Add a backup question or example in your lesson plan.
- Use body language as a signal to pause or pivot.
- Have an extension and a support option ready.
- Build in one mid-lesson check-in to see how students are doing.

Over time, these small habits sharpen your instincts—and adapting becomes second nature.

Let's Explore: 7 Adaptive Moves

On the following pages, we'll dive into seven teacher moves that help you stay flexible, respond in real time, and keep learning on track—no matter what the day throws your way:

Adjusting Pacing
Offering Multiple Explanations
Responding to Student Questioning
Circling Back
Stop and Reset
Reframing the Task
Task Reduction

Let's take a closer look at each.

Adjusting Pacing

Purpose:

To match the speed of instruction with students' needs, ensuring they have enough time to learn while maintaining engagement and momentum.

Description:

This strategy involves reading the room in real time and shifting the speed of instruction based on students' understanding, engagement, and readiness. By slowing down when students need more support or speeding up when they're ready, you create a balance that keeps everyone learning and engaged.

How to Use It:

1. Read the Room

Pay attention to body language, participation, and energy. Signs of confusion, restlessness, or disengagement often signal that pacing needs adjusting.

2. Slow It Down

When students are struggling, provide more time. Break concepts into smaller steps, add practice opportunities, or reteach with a different approach.

3. Pick Up the Pace

When students show mastery or enthusiasm, move forward. Offer enrichment activities, introduce the next concept, or allow advanced learners to dive deeper.

4. Check for Understanding in Real Time

Use quick polls, turn-and-talks, or mini whiteboard responses to see if students are ready to move on—or need more time.

Example: In music class, your students are practicing clapping rhythm patterns. You notice that while some keep the beat confidently, others struggle to stay on tempo. Instead of pushing ahead, you slow the rhythm down and break it into smaller chunks before rebuilding the full sequence. This gives all learners a chance to succeed before moving to the next challenge.

When to Use It:

- During instruction or review
- When students appear confused or need extra time to process
- When students demonstrate readiness to move ahead
- Anytime ongoing checks for understanding suggest a change of pace is needed

Why It Works:

- ✓ Keeps lessons responsive to student needs
- ✓ Reduces frustration and boredom
- ✓ Promotes mastery and confidence before moving on
- ✓ Encourages deeper engagement for all learners

Offering Multiple Explanations

Purpose:

To adapt instruction in real time by rephrasing or demonstrating concepts in different ways so all students can access the learning.

Description:

This strategy involves responding on the spot when students look confused or disengaged. Instead of repeating the same explanation, you shift your approach—using simpler language, visuals, analogies, or student input. Offering multiple explanations ensures that abstract or complex ideas become clearer, making learning more accessible to diverse learners.

How to Use It:

1. **Notice Signs of Confusion**

   Watch for blank stares, lack of participation, or repeated errors as cues that your first explanation didn't land.

2. **Reframe on the Spot**

   Restate the concept using different vocabulary, a concrete example, or a simpler model.

3. **Switch Modalities**

   Draw a quick diagram, use objects in the room, or connect the idea to a familiar situation.

4. **Invite Student Thinking**

   Ask a student to explain in their own words or pair up to teach it to a partner. Use their responses to add another layer of explanation.

Example: During a math lesson on fractions, you explain how ¼ is smaller than ½. Some students still look puzzled. You grab fraction tiles to model part-to-whole relationships, then sketch a number line on the board, and finally compare it to sharing slices of pizza. Each quick shift helps more students connect with the concept in real time.

When to Use It:

- When you notice confusion after your first explanation
- When students need immediate clarification of abstract ideas

Why It Works:

✓ Responsive to student needs in the moment
✓ Provides multiple pathways for understanding
✓ Reduces frustration and keeps students engaged
✓ Encourages flexibility and creativity in learning

Responding to Student Questions

Purpose:

To adapt instruction in the moment by honoring student curiosity and using their questions to deepen learning, strengthen connections, and make lessons more relevant.

Description:

This strategy involves pausing to validate and explore student questions. By honoring curiosity, you model inquiry, show respect for student thinking, and create opportunities to extend understanding. Thoughtful responses—whether immediate or delayed—help connect classroom content to the real world.

How to Use It:

1. Pause and Acknowledge

When a student asks a thoughtful question, stop briefly to validate their curiosity and signal that their thinking matters.

2. Connect to Learning Goals

Link the question back to the current lesson or use it as a natural bridge to introduce new content.

3. Encourage Collective Inquiry

Open the question to the class. Invite peers to share possible answers, ideas, or predictions.

4. Balance Timing

Decide whether to address the question right away, return to it later in the lesson, or weave it into future instruction.

Example: During a math lesson on perimeter, a student asks, "Does the area change if the perimeter is the same?" You pause and acknowledge the great question, then turn it back to the class: "What do you think? Can two shapes have the same perimeter but different areas?" Students sketch quick examples on whiteboards, compare answers with partners, and discover the relationship together before you connect it back to the learning goal.

When to Use It:

- When a student's question can clarify understanding
- When curiosity can be extended or deepened
- When the question can make the lesson more meaningful

Why It Works:

✓ Validates student voice and curiosity

✓ Strengthens relevance by linking content to the real world

✓ Encourages critical thinking and inquiry

✓ Builds a culture where questions drive learning

Circling Back

Purpose:

To provide multiple opportunities to reinforce learning before moving forward based on student readiness.

Description:

This strategy involves intentionally revisiting concepts when students show confusion or gaps in understanding. By circling back, you can address misconceptions, strengthen understanding, and give learners the confidence to build on solid foundations.

How to Use It:

1. **Check for Understanding**

   Use informal assessments, quizzes, or class discussions to identify areas where students are struggling.

2. **Plan Focused Reviews**

   Design short, targeted reviews that zero in on specific gaps rather than reteaching the entire lesson.

3. **Try a New Approach**

   Present the concept differently—through visuals, hands-on activities, or real-world examples.

4. **Reassess Progress**

   After circling back, use another quick check (discussion, problem, or reflection) to confirm that misconceptions have been cleared.

Example: After a science quiz reveals confusion about photosynthesis, you circle back by leading a hands-on demonstration: spinach leaves in water with baking soda are placed under a lamp, producing oxygen bubbles. Students observe the reaction, connect it to photosynthesis, and then create labeled diagrams to reinforce the concept before moving ahead.

When to Use It:

- After assessments reveal gaps or misconceptions
- During class discussions when confusion surfaces
- Anytime patterns of misunderstanding persist

Why It Works:

- ✓ Prevents learning gaps from compounding
- ✓ Reinforces key concepts with fresh approaches
- ✓ Boosts student confidence and mastery

Stop and Reset

Purpose:

To adapt instruction in the moment by shifting the activity or structure when students lose focus, energy dips, or learning is no longer productive.

Description:

This strategy involves pausing and pivoting to a new approach when the current activity isn't working. Instead of pushing through, you stop, reset expectations, and adjust the learning format. By resetting with intention, you re-engage students and create conditions for success.

How to Use It:

1. **Notice the Signals**

   Pay attention to disengagement, restlessness, or confusion. These cues suggest it's time to reset.

2. **Pause and Acknowledge**

   Stop the lesson briefly. Name what you're noticing in a calm, neutral tone.

3. **Reset Expectations**

   Explain the pivot and what the new structure will look like.

4. **Shift the Activity**

   Transition into the new format—independent work, partner talk, movement, or a different type of task.

5. **Restart with Purpose**

   Give students a clear entry point and encourage them to re-engage with focus and energy.

Example: During a math review game, students become overly competitive and noisy. You pause and say, "This isn't helping us focus on the math. Let's reset. Instead of teams, each of you will solve the next set of problems independently, and then we'll share strategies together." The class shifts to quiet practice and focus quickly returns.

When to Use It:

- When an activity becomes unproductive or off-task
- When energy levels are too high or too low
- When the current structure isn't supporting learning
- Anytime a pivot will restore focus and engagement

Why It Works:

✓ Prevents wasted time by adapting in real time
✓ Restores focus without escalating conflict
✓ Models flexibility and problem-solving
✓ Creates a fresh start that re-engages students

Reframing the Task

Purpose:

To re-engage students by shifting how a task is presented when the original framing leads to confusion, frustration, or disengagement.

Description:

This strategy involves offering a new entry point when the way a task is introduced creates unnecessary barriers. Reframing keeps the learning goal intact but makes the process more accessible, relevant, or motivating.

How to Use It:

1. **Notice Signs of Struggle**

   Pay attention to signs of frustration, distraction, or lack of progress.

2. **Adjust the Framing, Keep the Goal**

   Modify how students access the task while holding the same objective.

3. **Tap Into Interests**

   Connect the task to hobbies, experiences, or passions students already care about to boost motivation.

Example: Your students are struggling to write summaries of a nonfiction article. You reframe the task by saying, "Pretend you're telling a younger sibling or friend what this article is about in three simple sentences." With this new perspective, your students approach the task with less pressure and more clarity.

When to Use It:

- When students seem stuck, overwhelmed, or off-task
- When a task feels unclear or overly abstract
- When engagement is low and a fresh entry point is needed

Why It Works:

✓ Maintains rigor while reducing barriers

✓ Encourages flexible thinking by showing multiple ways to approach a problem

✓ Reignites interest and motivation

Task Reduction

Purpose:

To maintain high expectations while making learning more manageable for students who feel overwhelmed in the moment.

Description:

This strategy involves reducing the size or complexity of a task while keeping the learning goal intact. Task reduction helps students stay engaged by focusing on the essential skills or concepts without unnecessary barriers.

How to Use It:

1. **Identify the Essential Learning Goal**

   Ask yourself, "What's the most important skill or concept here?" Eliminate steps that don't directly support it.

2. **Chunk the Work**

   Break larger tasks into smaller, sequential steps. Release one piece at a time instead of the entire assignment.

3. **Offer Streamlined Choices**

   Provide a reduced set of problems, prompts, or examples while still allowing students to show understanding.

4. **Build Stamina Gradually**

   Begin with smaller tasks and increase length or complexity over time as confidence grows.

Example: In a math lesson on long division, you give students ten multi-step problems. One student shuts down, feeling overwhelmed. You reduce the task by saying, "Let's do one problem together, then you try two on your own." With fewer problems at a time, the student regains focus and successfully demonstrates the skill.

When to Use It:

- When students are overwhelmed or shutting down
- When frustration is blocking progress
- During independent work or homework assignment for students who require extra time

Why It Works:

- ✓ Keeps the learning goal intact
- ✓ Reduces cognitive overload
- ✓ Promotes perseverance and confidence

Final Thoughts

Adaptive moves are the heartbeat of responsive teaching. They're not about having the perfect plan. They're about knowing when to pause, pivot, and meet students where they are. When you adjust in real time—whether it's rephrasing a question, switching up the pacing, or taking a moment to reset—you show students that their needs matter.

These moves signal care, flexibility, and trust. You're saying, "I see you. I'm with you. Let's figure this out together."

Over time, adaptive teaching becomes less about reacting and more about *responding*—with intention, clarity, and calm. You build confidence in your ability to adjust, and your students build confidence knowing they're supported.

Adaptive moves don't just help students stay engaged and on track; they help you grow too. They keep your teaching fresh, reflective, and responsive to the students in front of you.

So, keep reading the room. Keep shifting when it counts. Every thoughtful adjustment moves you closer to a classroom that is inclusive, effective, and connected.

Up Next

While adaptive moves keep learning on track in the moment, they work best when they're built on a foundation of trust and emotional safety. Students are more willing to take risks, stay engaged, and bounce back from setbacks when they know their teacher sees them as more than just learners—they're people with feelings, challenges, and strengths.

That's where emotional support moves come in. In the next chapter, we'll explore how to create a classroom culture that not only supports academic growth but also nurtures the social and emotional well-being of every student.

PUTTING IT INTO PRACTICE

Now that you've seen the why and how behind effective adaptive moves, let's explore what they might look like in real life.

The following scenarios are pulled from common classroom moments—ones that every teacher has faced in some form. Each one invites you to pause, reflect, and consider:

What moves might I make in this moment?

This is where theory meets practice—and where your instincts and toolkit come together.

SCENARIOS

The Wi-Fi Wipeout

The Kindergarten Stand-Off

The Lesson That Fell Apart

Scenario 1: The Wi-Fi Wipeout

It's Friday morning in your grade 6 classroom, and you've just launched a tech-integrated language lesson. Students are excited. They'll be using tablets to collaborate on a shared Google Doc as they co-write short mystery stories in pairs.

You've modeled the process. Expectations are clear. Engagement is high.

And then—

The Wi-Fi drops.

At first, you think it's a quick glitch. But a double check confirms the worst: the entire school is offline, and no one knows for how long.

Within minutes:

- Students begin calling out: "It's not loading!" and "My doc's gone!"
- A few are poking around, trying to reconnect, while others are getting frustrated and off-task.
- Tyler announces, "Sweet! I guess we're not doing anything now."
- Amira looks panicked—she's been working hard on her writing and doesn't want to lose her work.

The momentum you built is slipping, and thirty-five minutes remain in the block. Your entire lesson hinged on the tech working. Now it's not.

You glance at the whiteboard. The anchor chart. The books on the shelf. Time to adapt.

How Might You Respond?

- How could you pivot quickly to keep the learning goals alive without the devices?
- What adaptive teacher moves could you use to maintain focus, minimize frustration, and make the most of the moment?
- How might you reframe the experience to model flexibility and resilience?

Scenario 2: The Kindergarten Stand-Off

It's center time in your kindergarten classroom. The room is abuzz with small groups playing, building, and exploring. You make your way over to the art table and remind a few students that it will be cleanup time in five minutes.

Most begin to wind down when the signal goes off—except for Jordan.

Jordan is seated at the sensory center, elbow-deep in dry rice and scoops. You crouch beside him and say gently, "Time to clean up, Jordan. Let's pour the rice back in together."

Without looking at you, he loudly protests, "No."

You smile, repeat the request gently and hold out your hand.

Jordan crosses his arms and growls: "I don't want to. You can't make me."

You pause. The energy in the room shifts. A few kids glance over to see what you'll do.

Jordan grabs another scoop of rice and dumps it slowly on the floor, staring right at you.

You know he's testing limits—but also that there's likely more beneath the surface.

You feel the pressure to respond calmly, firmly, and without turning it into a power struggle.

How Might You Respond?

- How would you handle Jordan's defiance in a way that preserves dignity and builds trust?
- What calming or connection-based moves could you use to de-escalate the moment?
- How can you balance structure with empathy in a high-emotion moment with a five-year-old?

Scenario 3: The Lesson That Fell Apart

It's a rainy Wednesday afternoon, and your grade 5 students have been indoors all day. No recess. No gym. You're halfway through a carefully planned social studies lesson about Canadian provinces and territories, using a slideshow, a map activity, and small group research stations.

But from the moment the lesson begins, things feel off.

- The projector won't turn on, so your anchor visuals are a no-go.
- The groups you formed are arguing over who does what, and two students are in tears after a disagreement.
- Dashawn keeps blurting out jokes to get laughs.
- Sana is quietly refusing to work with her partner.
- The energy is scattered, and no one seems focused. Even your normally reliable students are off task.
- You look at the clock. There are still forty minutes left, and your beautifully structured lesson is clearly not going to land today.

You feel the urge to push through, to stick to the plan. But something tells you that won't serve anyone.

You pause. Take a breath. It's time to pivot.

How Might You Respond?

- How would you adapt your approach in real time to meet students where they are?
- What quick adaptive moves could shift the energy, reset the tone, or salvage meaningful learning?
- How do you make space for flexibility without losing structure?

Chapter 8

Emotional Support Moves

"My teacher notices when I'm having a hard day. She doesn't make a big deal, just checks in." **—Grade 5 student**

Learning thrives in classrooms where students feel safe, respected, and valued. You can have the sharpest lesson plan, the clearest explanations, and the most engaging activities—but if a student feels anxious, invisible, or disconnected, they won't be fully present.

That's where emotional support moves come in. These are the intentional choices you make to create a classroom environment where students feel seen, valued, and cared for. Emotional support isn't about fixing students' problems. It's about showing up with empathy, creating consistency, and building trust.

You don't need to have all the answers. You just need to lead with humanity.

You can't always fix the problem, but you can be the steady presence in the middle of it.

Why These Moves Matter

Students don't leave their emotions at the door. They bring their full selves—joy, anxiety, frustration, curiosity, fear, excitement—into your classroom. Emotional support moves ensure that the classroom remains a safe place to be themselves, even on hard days.

Strong emotional support moves allow you to:

- Build trust and strengthen relationships.

- Teach emotional regulation skills.
- Maintain a calm, respectful classroom culture.
- Support students through challenges both in and out of school.
- Lay the groundwork for stronger academic performance.

Students won't remember every lesson, but they'll remember how you made them feel.

So, What Are Emotional Support Moves?

Emotional support moves are the daily actions and responses you use to care for your students' emotional well-being. Some are built into your classroom routines, like greeting students at the door or using mindfulness to start the day. Others happen in the moment, like checking in after a tough interaction or using empowering language to help a student reset.

Think of emotional support moves as the foundation under every other teaching move. They help students regulate their emotions, take academic risks, and build positive relationships—with you and with each other.

Emotional support is core to effective teaching.

What Makes These Moves Work?

At their heart, emotional support moves are about helping students feel safe, supported, and connected. They:

Build Trust

Students know they can count on you, not just for learning, but for understanding and support. That trust creates the foundation.

Promote Emotional Regulation

You help students notice, name, and navigate their feelings in healthy ways—whether through tools, modeling, or reflection.

Foster Inclusivity

You create a space where all students feel respected and valued, no matter their background.

Encourage Resilience

You frame mistakes as learning opportunities and celebrate persistence.

Before students can learn, they need to feel safe. Because emotions and learning are deeply connected, engagement suffers when students feel unseen or unsettled.

The most effective emotional support moves share these qualities:

- **Proactive** — You build routines and rituals that make students feel secure before challenges arise.
- **Responsive** — You notice cues like posture, tone, silence, or energy shifts, and respond with care.
- **Nonjudgmental** — You meet mistakes with empathy, not shame, offering understanding and clear boundaries.
- **Developmentally Appropriate** — You adapt your approach for the age and needs of your students.
- **Consistent** — You show up the same way—calm, compassionate, and steady—so students know what to expect.

These moves aren't about fixing every problem. They're about showing students they matter and that the classroom is a place they can count on.

When you lead with empathy, stay grounded, and build systems that support emotional well-being, you're not just managing behavior. You're modeling what it means to be a steady, caring presence in a world that can sometimes feel anything but.

Real Talk: What This Looks Like in Action

A student walks in clearly upset. They're withdrawn, distracted, and tense.

What do you do?

- You greet them by name and quietly check in at their desk—***private check-in move.***
- You offer a mindfulness activity to help them regulate—***self-regulation move.***
- You say, "I'm glad you're here. It's okay to have hard days."—***empathy statement move.***
- You adjust your expectations for that moment and celebrate a small step forward—***celebrating small wins move.***

These moments might seem small, but they matter. They create connection. They build trust. They make space for learning.

Your consistency is their security.

You Don't Have to Be a Therapist

You're a teacher, not a therapist. But emotional support moves aren't about solving everything. They're about being the adult in the room who sees, listens, and shows care.

Start small:

- Greet students by name.
- Use one empathy-based phrase a day.
- Celebrate effort, not just achievement.
- Include a brief mindfulness check-in.
- Keep simple regulation tools handy.

The goal is presence; the steady reminder to students that someone sees them, cares for them, and believes they belong.

Let's Explore: 14 Emotional Support Moves

On the following pages, we'll explore fourteen teacher moves that help build emotional safety, foster resilience, and support students in becoming confident, emotionally aware learners:

Creating a Safe Space
Mindfulness Practices
Daily Affirmations
Practicing Gratitude
Emotional Labeling
Self-Regulation Tools
Acknowledging Effort
Normalizing Mistakes
Celebrating Small Wins
Private Check-Ins
Empathy Statements
Empowering Language
Good News Visits
Positive Communication Home

Let's take a closer look at each.

Creating a Safe Space

Purpose:

To build and maintain a classroom environment where every student feels emotionally safe, respected, and valued.

Description:

This strategy involves nurturing emotional safety daily through your words, actions, and responses. When you create a safe classroom space, you give students permission to show up fully as themselves. This encourages risk-taking, fosters belonging, and supports social-emotional growth—making academic and personal learning more meaningful and accessible for your students.

How to Use It:

1. Establish Clear Norms

At the start of the year (and revisit often), co-create community agreements focused on respect, kindness, and listening to understand. Post these norms visibly and model them consistently.

2. Respond to Disrespect Immediately

If hurtful comments or exclusion happen, step in calmly and constructively. Use language that redirects behavior without shaming.

- "In our classroom, we speak to each other with kindness. Let's try that again."

3. Encourage Open Dialogue

Give students regular chances to share their thoughts, feelings, and perspectives. Try community circles, discussion prompts, or reflection journals to build trust and normalize diverse opinions.

4. Validate All Voices

Show students their contributions matter by saying things like:

- "Thank you for sharing that."
- "That's an important point we need to consider."

Acknowledge differing views while reinforcing respect.

5. **Model Vulnerability and Growth**

   Demonstrate that it's okay to make mistakes, change your mind, or not have all the answers. When you show humility, students see that learning matters more than perfection.

Example: During a classroom debate, students begin interrupting and dismissing each other's ideas. You pause the conversation and say, "Let's remember that disagreement is part of learning, but respect is non-negotiable." You lead a quick reset, revisit discussion norms, and then restart the debate. Students continue with a renewed focus on listening and kindness.

When to Use It:

- Always—practice continuously
- During sensitive or challenging discussions
- When resolving conflict
- Anytime students are trying new or difficult tasks

Why It Works:

✓ Builds trust and belonging
✓ Encourages student voice and risk-taking
✓ Creates a culture of respect and empathy
✓ Promotes equity and inclusion

Mindfulness Practices

Purpose:

To help students regulate emotions, manage stress, and improve focus.

Description:

This strategy involves integrating mindfulness into daily routines using simple, consistent practices that build self-awareness. These practices help students feel calmer, more focused, and ready to engage in learning. Over time, this fosters a classroom culture of balance and emotional safety.

How to Use It:

1. Start with Simple Techniques

Begin your day or lesson with brief activities like breathing exercises, body scans, or quiet moments of reflection. Keep them short and accessible for everyone.

2. Teach Self-Regulation Tools

Show students strategies they can use independently, such as:

- deep breathing
- grounding techniques (e.g., '5-4-3-2-1' senses check)
- silent counting

Encourage them to use these tools when they feel stressed, anxious, or frustrated.

3. Use Mindfulness for Transitions

Build in quick mindfulness breaks between activities to reset focus. For example, after recess or gym, use a calming routine to help students shift back into learning mode.

4. Normalize Emotional Check-Ins

Invite students to share how they're feeling with simple tools like mood meters, hand signals, or one-word check-ins. Use what they share to adjust the classroom tone and provide support.

5. **Model Mindfulness**

   Participate in mindfulness activities alongside students to show that mindfulness is for everyone—not just kids. By participating, you normalize the practice and build credibility.

Example: Before a challenging math test, you notice students fidgeting and whispering anxiously. You pause and lead them in a **box-breathing** exercise: inhale for four counts, hold for four counts, exhale for four counts, hold for four counts. After a few rounds, the room grows calmer, and students begin the test with a more focused mindset.

When to Use It:

- Before assessments or stressful tasks
- After high-energy activities or transitions
- When the classroom feels unsettled
- Anytime students need help managing emotions
- Regularly, to build lifelong habits for focus and calm

Why It Works:

✓ Promotes emotional regulation

✓ Improves focus and readiness to learn

✓ Builds long-term coping strategies for stress

Daily Affirmations

Purpose:

To help students build confidence, reduce anxiety, and develop a growth mindset.

Description:

This strategy involves using short, empowering statements that remind students that effort, kindness, and resilience matter. Over time, affirmations strengthen self-belief and create a classroom culture of encouragement and belonging.

How to Use It:

1. Choose Simple, Positive Statements

Select affirmations that are age-appropriate, encouraging, and focused on growth. Examples include:

- "I can try new things, even if they're hard."
- "I am kind and helpful."
- "Mistakes help me grow."

2. Say Them Aloud Together

Begin the day—or reset after transitions—by reciting affirmations as a class. Use call-and-response, choral reading, or mirror talk, where students repeat affirmations while looking at themselves or making eye contact with you.

3. Rotate and Personalize

Change affirmations regularly to keep them fresh and meaningful. Invite students to suggest affirmations or write their own to build ownership.

4. Model Belief in the Words

Say affirmations with energy and sincerity. Show students how you use affirmations yourself—before a test, after a mistake, or during a tough moment.

Example: Each morning, you gather your class in a circle and lead them in saying: "Today, I will try my best. I am capable, I am learning, and I belong here." Afterward, everyone takes a deep breath and starts the day with calm focus and confidence.

When to Use It:

- At the start of the day
- Before assessments or challenges
- After transitions
- Anytime students need emotional grounding

Why It Works:

- ✓ Builds student confidence
- ✓ Creates a positive classroom climate
- ✓ Promotes resilience and self-belief

Practicing Gratitude

Purpose:

To help students focus on the positive, regulate emotions, and strengthen relationships.

Description:

This strategy involves creating opportunities for students to reflect on what they are thankful for. This helps them shift attention away from stress or frustration and toward positivity. Gratitude fosters empathy, appreciation, and a sense of belonging in the classroom community.

How to Use It:

1. Create a Daily or Weekly Gratitude Routine

Set aside a few minutes for students to write or share something they're grateful for. You can build this into morning meetings, journal time, or end-of-day reflections.

2. Model Specific Gratitude

Teach students to go beyond general statements like "I'm thankful for everything." Show them how to be specific:

- "I'm grateful that my friend included me at recess today."
- "I'm thankful my teacher helped me when I got stuck in math."

3. Use Different Formats

Mix it up. Students can share aloud, write in journals, add to a class gratitude jar, or post sticky notes on a "Gratitude Wall." Keep it flexible and low-pressure.

4. Connect to Social-Emotional Growth

Talk about how noticing small positives improves mood, reduces stress, and helps us get through tough times.

Example: At the end of each day, you ask students to jot one thing they're grateful for on a sticky note. They can keep it private or add it to the class "Gratitude Wall." Over time, the wall fills with moments of kindness, small wins, and connections that remind everyone of what's going well.

When to Use It:

- During morning meetings
- As part of end-of-day reflections
- After stressful events or conflicts
- Anytime the class needs a mindset reset

Why It Works:

- ✓ Shifts focus from stress to positivity
- ✓ Promotes empathy and appreciation
- ✓ Builds resilience and emotional regulation

Emotional Labeling

Purpose:

To help students build emotional awareness and regulation by learning how to identify and name their feelings.

Description:

This strategy involves teaching students the language of emotions and giving them tools to express themselves with clarity. When students can label emotions, they're better able to manage them in healthy and productive ways. This builds empathy, strengthens relationships, and supports self-regulation, creating a classroom culture where feelings are acknowledged and respected.

How to Use It:

1. Teach Emotion Vocabulary

Go beyond the basics like *happy, sad,* or *mad.* Introduce words such as *frustrated, worried, proud, calm, or curious* so students can describe their emotions more precisely.

2. Model Emotional Labeling

Use "I" statements throughout the day. For example:

- "I'm feeling a little nervous about trying something new, but I'm also excited to learn."

3. Create Safe Opportunities to Share

Build moments into morning meetings or check-ins where students can share feelings. Use sentence starters like:

- "Today I feel _____ because _____."

4. Use Visual Supports

Post emotion charts or mood meters on the wall. Invite students to point to or select feelings when they don't have the words yet.

5. Normalize All Emotions

Reassure students that all feelings are okay—it's what we do with them that matters. Validate their experiences without judgment. Say things like:

- "It's okay to feel frustrated. What matters is what we do next."

Example: Before group work begins, you notice some students look uneasy. You pause and say, "Let's do a quick check. Who's feeling excited? Who's feeling a little worried about working in a group? Both are normal. Let's talk about how we can work together even with different feelings." This quick reset helps students name emotions and move forward more effectively.

When to Use It:

- During morning meetings or check-ins
- When facilitating conflict resolution
- During pivotal moments
- Anytime students seem overwhelmed or disconnected

Why It Works:

✓ Builds emotional awareness

✓ Promotes empathy and understanding

✓ Supports regulation and resilience

Self-Regulation Tools

Purpose:

To help students learn how to manage their emotions, refocus independently, and build resilience.

Description:

This strategy involves providing students with tools and teaching them how to use them, giving them the ability to reset without relying solely on you. These tools create a sense of ownership, build lifelong coping skills, and support a classroom climate where everyone can stay engaged in learning.

How to Use It:

1. Create a Calm Space

Set up a "calm corner" or "reset station" in your classroom. Stock it with simple, non-disruptive tools like stress balls, fidget items, sensory bottles, breathing cards, or coloring sheets. Post a visual guide or checklist so students know how to choose a strategy.

2. Model and Teach Skills

Don't wait until students are upset to introduce tools. Practice strategies as a class—such as deep breathing, mindful pauses, or stretching—so students know what to do when emotions rise.

3. Encourage Self-Awareness

Teach students to notice signs they need a break. Use prompts like:

- "How is your body feeling right now?"
- "Would a calming strategy help you get back on track?"

4. **Normalize and Reinforce Use**

   Treat self-regulation as a skill, not a consequence. Acknowledge when students use tools effectively:

   - "I'm proud of you for noticing you needed a break before you got too frustrated."

5. **Plan for Return**

   Set expectations for how long students use the calm space and what happens afterward (e.g., checking in with you briefly and then rejoining the activity).

Example: During a math lesson, a student gets stuck and starts to feel upset. You quietly say, "I can see this is frustrating. Would you like to use the calm corner for a few minutes to reset?" The student spends five minutes using a glitter jar for breathing focus before returning to the task with a calmer mindset.

When to Use It:

- When students feel overwhelmed, frustrated, anxious, or disengaged
- During classroom transitions
- After conflicts or emotional upsets
- While teaching or reinforcing social-emotional skills

Why It Works:

✓ Builds independence and resilience

✓ Strengthens emotional regulation skills

✓ Allows for individual needs to be met while maintaining classroom flow

Acknowledging Effort

Purpose:

To reinforce a growth mindset by highlighting effort.

Description:

This strategy involves celebrating students' persistence, improvement, and dedication. When you recognize the hard work behind the learning process, you shift the focus from perfection to progress. Students begin to value the strategies they use, which fosters resilience and long-term motivation.

How to Use It:

1. Be Specific

Point out the exact behaviors or actions that show effort. Instead of saying, "Good job," try:

- "I noticed you kept working on your writing even when it got tricky."

2. Highlight the Process

Draw attention to what students *did*—like revising, trying a new method, or asking for help—so they see the value in **how** they learn, not just in getting the answer right.

3. Praise Progress, Not Just Perfection

Recognize small steps forward, such as clearer handwriting, stronger teamwork, or more detailed questions—even if the final goal hasn't been met yet.

4. Encourage Reflection

After giving feedback, prompt students to think about their effort:

- "What strategy helped you make progress today?"
- "What part are you proud of?"

Example: During basketball, a student has trouble making baskets but diligently practices dribbling and shooting every class. You say, "I noticed how you kept adjusting your stance and trying again—you didn't give up. That persistence is helping you improve your control of the ball."

When to Use It:

- When students are showing persistence, even if they haven't met the goal yet
- During long-term projects or skill-building tasks
- When students feel stuck, frustrated, or doubtful about their abilities
- Anytime you want to encourage resilience and perseverance

Why It Works:

✓ Builds confidence and motivation

✓ Reinforces a growth mindset

✓ Helps students see learning as progress, not perfection

Normalizing Mistakes

Purpose:

To create a classroom culture where mistakes are valued as part of the learning process. By showing students that errors are opportunities for growth, you help them build resilience, persistence, and confidence.

Description:

This strategy involves removing the fear of being wrong and replacing it with curiosity and problem-solving. This approach encourages students to take risks, reflect on their learning, and view challenges as steps toward mastery.

How to Use It:

1. **Model Making Mistakes**

   Show students that adults make mistakes too. Say them aloud and demonstrate how to respond:

   - "I mixed up the steps—let me try again. That's how we learn!"

2. **Celebrate Productive Struggle**

   Praise effort, not just correctness. Use phrases like:

   - "I love how you stuck with that, even when you were unsure."

3. **Deconstruct Errors Together**

   Treat mistakes as teachable moments. Ask, "What can we learn from this mistake?" rather than, "Who got it right?"

4. **Use Growth-Oriented Language**

   Replace phrases like "wrong answer" with supportive phrases such as:

   - "This didn't work—yet"

5. **Create Safety Around Risk-Taking**

   Share stories of famous inventors, writers, or athletes who failed before succeeding. Emphasize that trying again is what leads to improvement.

Example: During a health lesson, a student answers a question incorrectly and looks embarrassed. You respond, "Thank you for being brave and sharing your thinking. Mistakes help us see how to grow. Let's work through this together."

When to Use It:

- During practice or problem-solving activities
- When introducing new or challenging concepts
- In creative tasks that require risk-taking
- Anytime students seem afraid to share ideas or answers

Why It Works:

- ✓ Builds resilience and persistence
- ✓ Reduces fear of failure
- ✓ Encourages risk-taking and deeper learning
- ✓ Fosters a growth mindset

Celebrating Small Wins

Purpose:

To help students build confidence, resilience, and a sense of achievement by recognizing progress along the way.

Description:

This strategy involves acknowledging small wins and helping students see that each step forward matters. By celebrating incremental growth—not just results—you reinforce persistence and show that effort and improvement are valued. This practice motivates them to keep trying, builds momentum, and cultivates a classroom culture where progress is celebrated.

How to Use It:

1. **Notice the Small Steps**

   Pay attention to moments when students try something new, stick with a challenge, or improve even slightly—such as completing work independently, participating more, or attempting a tough skill.

2. **Give Meaningful Praise**

   Make your feedback specific and genuine. Instead of "Good job," say:

   - "You used complete sentences in your journal entry today. That's a big improvement from last week."

3. **Use Varied Acknowledgment**

   Choose methods that fit the situation:

   - Verbal praise
   - Sticky notes or quick messages
   - Stickers, points, or tokens
   - Adding names to a recognition board

4. **Make It Visible or Personal**

   Decide whether to recognize the win publicly or privately. A class shout-out may motivate some students, while others may appreciate a quiet word or written note.

Example: During independent reading, a student who usually struggles to stay focused reads quietly for ten minutes without distraction. You say, "I noticed you stayed focused the whole time today—that's big improvement."

When to Use It:

- Throughout the day to encourage persistence
- When students are building new habits
- During long-term projects or skill development
- With students who need extra motivation or reassurance

Why It Works:

✓ Builds confidence and motivation

✓ Reinforces the value of persistence

✓ Creates momentum toward bigger goals

✓ Helps students feel seen and appreciated

Private Check-Ins

Purpose:

To strengthen relationships and show students that you care about them beyond academics.

Description:

This strategy involves building personal connections with students by taking time to connect one-on-one about their well-being, feelings, or concerns. These check-ins foster trust and create a safe space for students to share what's on their minds.

How to Use It:

1. Be Observant

Pay attention to changes in mood, behavior, or participation. Withdrawal, frustration, or unusual quietness may be signs a student needs support.

2. Schedule Time Intentionally

Find natural moments—before school, after class, during independent work, or at dismissal—to have quick one-on-one conversations. Even two minutes can make a difference.

3. Ask Open-Ended Questions

Encourage dialogue with prompts such as:

- "How are things going for you today?"
- "Is there anything on your mind?"

Avoid yes/no questions that can shut down conversation.

4. Listen Without Judgment

Focus on listening more than fixing. Let students share at their own pace and validate their feelings without rushing to offer solutions.

5. **Follow Up**

   Revisit the conversation later to check how the student is doing. Consistency shows genuine care and helps build trust over time.

Example: A student who usually speaks up in discussions has been quiet all week. After class, you gently say, "I've noticed you've been a little quieter lately. Is something on your mind?" The student shares they're stressed about a family situation. You listen, reassure them, and connect them with support if needed.

When to Use It:

- When you notice changes in behavior, mood, or engagement
- During times of visible stress, conflict, or disengagement
- As part of building a caring and supportive classroom culture
- As a proactive practice to connect with all students

Why It Works:

✓ Builds trust and rapport
✓ Helps students feel valued beyond academics
✓ Provides insight into hidden struggles
✓ Creates a safe, supportive classroom climate

Empathy Statements

Purpose:

To help students feel seen, heard, and supported by acknowledging and validating their emotions.

Description:

This strategy involves noticing emotions and responding with compassion to show students that their feelings matter. Empathy statements shift the focus from fixing problems right away to first understanding and honoring what students are experiencing. Using empathetic language builds trust, deepens relationships, and creates a safe space for learning.

How to Use It:

1. Notice Emotional Cues

Pay attention to tone of voice, body language, or sudden changes in behavior that may signal frustration, embarrassment, or anxiety.

2. Acknowledge Emotions Openly

Use statements that reflect back the student's feelings without dismissing or minimizing them. For example:

- "It sounds like you're really frustrated with how that went."
- "I can tell this is important to you."

3. Keep the Focus on Listening

Allow students to share more before offering solutions. Sometimes, being heard is the support they need most.

4. Reframe Challenges as Opportunities

Once emotions are acknowledged, gently guide students toward next steps:

- "It's okay to feel stuck sometimes—let's figure out what might help."

5. **Model Empathy Regularly**

   Use empathetic language in academic and social settings so students see empathy as part of daily classroom culture.

Example: A student forgets their lines during play rehearsal and looks embarrassed. You respond, "I get why you're feeling embarrassed—that's a tough moment. But remember, everyone here is learning, and mistakes are part of the process. Let's practice together so you feel more confident next time."

When to Use It:

- When students feel frustrated, anxious, or disappointed
- In moments of nervousness or excitement
- Anytime a student needs reassurance or validation
- After assessments or public performances

Why It Works:

✓ Builds trust and emotional safety

✓ Shows students their feelings are valued

✓ Strengthens teacher-student relationships

✓ Encourages resilience and self-awareness

Empowering Language

Purpose:

To help students develop a positive, growth-oriented mindset.

Description:

This strategy involves using intentional language to shape how students see themselves as learners. By focusing on effort, strategy, and progress rather than perfection or fixed traits, empowering language fosters persistence, confidence, and resilience. When students hear affirming messages that normalize struggle and emphasize learning as a process, they begin to internalize the belief that they can grow through effort and experience.

How to Use It:

1. Reframe Mistakes as Learning Opportunities

Swap deficit statements like, "This is a bit challenging for you," for growth language:

- "You're still learning this skill, and that's okay."

2. Celebrate Effort and Strategy

Praise the process, not just the outcome. Say things like:

- "I can see how much effort you put into this."
- "Your approach to solving that problem was creative."

3. Use Action-Focused Feedback

Instead of labeling students, "You're a great writer," point out specific actions:

- "You used strong descriptive words in your story today."

4. Normalize Struggle

Remind students that challenges are part of learning. Use phrases like:

- "This is tricky, but you're building new skills by sticking with it."
- "You don't have it yet—but you will."

5. **Encourage Reflection**

   When mistakes happen, guide students to think forward:

   - "What did you try here?
   - "What could you do differently next time?"

Example: During a writing assignment, a student says, "I'm just bad at writing introductions." You respond, "You're not bad—you're still practicing. I noticed how your second draft was clearer than your first, which shows your revision strategy is working. Each time you practice, you're building the skills to write stronger openings."

When to Use It:

- During feedback and coaching moments
- When students show frustration or self-doubt
- While introducing new or challenging concepts
- During assessments or long-term projects
- Anytime fixed-mindset language shows up

Why It Works:

✓ Builds confidence and resilience

✓ Reinforces a growth mindset

✓ Encourages persistence through challenges

✓ Helps students see effort as a pathway to success

Good News Visits

Purpose:

To celebrate students' successes by giving them the chance to share positive moments with administrators, other teachers, or trusted adults.

Description:

This strategy involves spotlighting effort, growth, and kindness—not just big achievements—by sharing students' successes beyond the classroom. It helps students feel proud of their progress and shows them that their actions matter to the wider school community. These visits boost confidence, reinforce positive behavior, and strengthen connections across the school community.

How to Use It:

1. Spot the Moment

Notice when students demonstrate growth, perseverance, or kindness. Highlight these moments as "good news" worth sharing.

2. Prepare the Student

Guide students in practicing what they'll say. For example:

- "I met my writing goal today."
- "I helped my friend at recess."

4. Coordinate with Other Adults

Let administrators, office staff, or colleagues know about this practice so they can greet students warmly and reinforce the celebration.

5. Keep It Brief and Positive

Good news visits should be short and uplifting. The focus is on affirming effort, progress, or kindness—not only academic outcomes.

6. Follow Up

After the visit, check in with the student about how it felt to share their success and encourage them to keep working toward their next goal.

Example: During a reading group, a student who has struggled with decoding reads a full page independently. You say, "That's a huge accomplishment—let's go share it with the principal!" The student proudly reads a line in the office, and the principal celebrates their progress, making the achievement even more meaningful.

When to Use It:

- When students achieve personal milestones
- After a breakthrough or moment of perseverance
- To reinforce kindness or positive behavior
- When you want to spotlight students who aren't often recognized publicly

Why It Works:

✓ Builds student confidence and pride
✓ Reinforces positive behavior and growth
✓ Strengthens school-wide community connections
✓ Helps all students feel valued and seen

Positive Communication Home

Purpose:

To build strong school-home partnerships by sharing positive updates about students' effort, growth, and character.

Description:

This strategy involves shifting the narrative from problems to progress by proactively reaching out to families with positive news. When communication focuses on strengths—not just challenges—students are more motivated, and families feel like valued partners in the learning process.

How to Use It:

1. Spot Meaningful Moments

Look for times when students show persistence, kindness, improvement, or leadership. Small wins often mean the most when shared with families.

2. Choose the Right Method

Send notes, emails, postcards, or make phone calls. Pick the method that feels most natural and accessible for you and the family.

3. Be Specific and Sincere

Go beyond general praise. Instead of, "Mikayla was great today," say:

- "Mikayla jumped in to help a classmate during math, and her teamwork really made a difference."

4. Include the Student

Tell students when you plan to share their good news:

- "I'm so proud of how you handled that. I'm going to let your parents know tonight."

This reinforces the recognition and builds pride.

5. **Make It Routine**

   Set a weekly goal (for example, three families each week). Track your contacts so every student gets positive communication over time.

Example: A student who usually struggles with focus stays on task during writing. You send home, "Keegan stayed focused the entire writing block today and wrote a strong opening sentence. His effort really paid off. We're proud of him!"

When to Use It:

- Regularly throughout the school year
- After moments of growth, persistence, or kindness
- To spotlight students who don't often hear about their successes
- As part of a consistent routine for all students

Why It Works:

✓ Strengthens family-school trust

✓ Reinforces student confidence and effort

✓ Builds a positive, supportive community

✓ Helps families feel included in their child's learning journey

Final Thoughts

Emotional support moves don't require extra time, special training, or a perfect script. What they *do* require is presence, empathy, and intention. When you show up consistently with care—whether through a quiet check-in, a kind word, or a calming routine—you build something powerful: a classroom where students feel safe enough to be themselves and brave enough to learn.

These moments of connection don't just support emotional well-being—they unlock engagement, resilience, and a sense of belonging. When students feel emotionally grounded, they can take academic risks, recover from setbacks, and build stronger relationships with others.

The truth is, your emotional support moves might be the thing a student remembers most—not the lesson content, but *how you made them feel*. That feeling of being seen, supported, and believed in? It lasts.

Keep showing up. Keep creating calm. Keep leading with empathy. When you do, you're not just supporting learners—you're helping young people grow into resilient, compassionate human beings.

And that's a move that matters.

Up Next

Just as students grow when they feel supported, teachers grow when they pause to reflect. The work you've done to create a safe, caring space sets the stage for another essential practice: looking inward.

Reflective moves help you examine what's working, what needs adjusting, and how your choices impact learning.

In the next chapter, we'll explore how to turn everyday teaching moments into opportunities for insight, growth, and continuous improvement—for you and for your students.

PUTTING IT INTO PRACTICE

Now that you've seen the why and how behind effective emotional support moves, let's explore what they might look like in real life.

The following scenarios are pulled from common classroom moments—ones that every teacher has faced in some form. Each one invites you to pause, reflect, and consider:

What moves might I make in this moment?

This is where theory meets practice—and where your instincts and toolkit come together.

SCENARIOS

Tears at the Desk

I'm Just Stupid

The Music Meltdown

Scenario 1: Tears at the Desk

It's a regular Thursday morning in your grade 3 class. Students are settled into their morning routine—quiet work, soft music, and the hum of pencils moving across the page.

As you make your way around the room checking in, you notice Emily sitting perfectly still at her desk. Her head is down. Her pencil is untouched. Her paper is blank.

You crouch beside her and gently ask,

"Are you okay?"

She nods, barely. But when she looks up, her eyes are full of tears.

You wait a moment. Then she whispers:

"My dog died last night."

Your heart sinks. You know how much she loved that dog. She talked about him all the time.

You glance around the room. Other students are focused. The day's lessons still lie ahead. But right now, none of that feels as important as this moment.

You know the lesson can wait. You also know Emily may not have the words—or the emotional tools—to get through the morning on her own.

She looks at you, trying to hold it together, waiting for your next move.

How Might You Respond?

- How can you provide emotional support that is quiet, respectful, and safe?
- What teacher moves might help Emily feel seen and cared for without drawing unwanted attention?
- How might you balance her need for space or comfort while still managing the classroom?

Scenario 2: I'm Just Stupid

It's math time in your grade 4 classroom, and students are working independently on multi-step word problems. The room is relatively calm, with most students focused and quietly asking for help when needed.

But at the back table, Casden is sitting rigid in his chair, pencil clenched tightly in his fist. His paper is blank except for the first question—which has been erased several times, leaving the paper worn thin.

You approach and kneel beside him.

"Want to work through the first one together?" you offer.

He shakes his head.

You try again:

"I've seen you do this before. Let's just start with one part."

He mutters, barely above a whisper:

"What's the point? I'm just stupid."

The words land like a punch to the chest.

You pause. You know this isn't just about math. You've seen Casden get easily frustrated before—especially when tasks feel hard. But today, this is something deeper. It's a belief, a story he's starting to tell himself.

He avoids eye contact, shrinks into his hoodie, and shrugs. He's shutting down before he even tries.

How Might You Respond?

- What emotional support moves can help Casden reframe this moment and himself?
- How do you acknowledge his feelings without reinforcing them?
- How can you build his confidence over time while addressing the immediate situation with care?

Scenario 3: The Music Meltdown

It's Monday afternoon, and your grade 2 class is heading into music class with their usual mix of excitement and noise. Today's plan is to learn a simple rhythm pattern using hand drums and shakers.

You set the expectations clearly: "We'll listen first, then try it together."

You demonstrate the rhythm and invite students to echo it back using claps first.

Most students are engaged—some a little too enthusiastically.

But Shayla, who has been having a tough week, immediately bangs on her drum as loudly as possible, even while you're still giving instructions. You pause and remind everyone to wait.

Shayla smirks. Then hits it again. This time, faster. Louder.

You give her a gentle but firm cue:

"Shayla, please stop. We'll all play together in a moment."

She glares at you, crosses her arms, and mutters, "This is dumb. I hate music anyway."

A few students nearby giggle. One nervously moves her drum away from her. The rhythm exercise hasn't even begun, and the group energy is already unraveling.

You know Shayla sometimes struggles with emotional regulation and attention, but this is quickly becoming a disruption for the entire class. You also know this moment could either go downhill fast or be redirected.

How Might You Respond?

- How can you respond in a way that sets clear boundaries but still supports Shayla emotionally?
- What teacher moves might help you preserve the lesson flow while calming the room?
- How can you adjust in the moment to protect the learning environment for all students?

Chapter 9

Reflective Moves

> *"I started asking myself, 'Who's doing most of the talking in my class?' That one question changed everything."* —**Grade 6 teacher**

Great teaching doesn't happen by chance—it's built.

Not overnight, but over time, through trial, adjustment, and reflection. You teach. You notice what worked, and what didn't. Then you tweak, shift, and try again.

That's where reflective moves come in. These are the intentional practices you use to step back, take stock, and refine your approach. They're not about being critical. They're about being curious. Reflective teaching is how good teachers become *great* teachers.

Why These Moves Matter

You already know that students grow when they reflect on their learning. The same is true for teachers. Reflective moves help you stay intentional, grounded, and focused on what matters most: student growth and teacher growth—together.

Students grow when they reflect on their learning.
Teachers grow when they reflect on their teaching.

Strong reflective moves allow you to:

- Make data-informed decisions about instruction.
- Identify and amplify what's working.

- Spot patterns in student engagement or struggle.
- Continuously improve your teaching practice.
- Stay connected to your purpose and professional values.

So, What Are Reflective Moves?

Reflective moves are strategies you use to analyze your teaching methods, your classroom culture, and your impact. Some are routine, like reviewing exit tickets or jotting notes for yourself after a lesson. Others are deeper, like inviting student feedback, observing a colleague teach, or examining your classroom data with fresh eyes.

Think of them as your professional mirror. They help you see what's working, what needs a shift, and what small changes can lead to big impact.

Reflection isn't a one-time event. It's a habit.

The best reflection happens in conversation, not in isolation.

When the Teacher Isn't the Expert

During my fifth year of teaching, I started at a new school in a grade 3 classroom. The transition seemed straightforward until I realized I'd also inherited part of the previous teacher's assignment: teaching grade 8 music twice a week.

Let me be clear, I had ***no*** background in music. The teacher before me happened to have a strong personal passion for it. She could read music, played several instruments, and while she didn't have formal qualifications in the subject, she managed the grade 8 music curriculum with ease. It worked for her. So, whether by oversight or design, the timetable stayed the same, and I was expected to slide right in.

I was overwhelmed from day one. I tried to "fake it till I made it," but it didn't take long to realize that several students knew far more about music theory and reading notes than I did. Every time the class rolled around, I felt anxious. The stress of trying to teach something I didn't fully understand was taking a toll and I knew I couldn't keep it up for an entire school year.

I needed to pause and reflect.

I realized two things. First, I was good at connecting with students and creating a fun, inclusive learning environment. Second, I didn't have to be the expert in the room—because some of my students already were.

I reached out to the school's band teacher, who generously shared resources and simple, engaging activities I could use. I also empowered my musically inclined students to take on leadership roles. They helped demonstrate skills, explain concepts, and guide their classmates through the technical parts I couldn't teach myself. I made it clear to my students that I didn't know everything and that we would figure it out together.

That shift changed everything. What started as a class I dreaded became one that I (slowly, over time) came to enjoy. Students stepped up, leaned in, and took pride in teaching and learning from one another. And I learned that reflection isn't just about fixing problems. It's about recognizing your strengths, leaning into them, and being open to doing things differently.

That year reminded me that we don't have to know it all. We just need to be willing to reflect, adapt, and let students be part of the solution.

What Makes These Moves Work?

At their core, reflective moves help you grow—and help your students thrive because of it.

Reflective moves:

Promote Growth

Identify what's working, where you can stretch, and how to move forward with purpose.

Enhance Student Learning

Refine instruction based on feedback and results so it stays relevant and effective.

Foster Professional Development

Build habits that help you adapt, improve, and stay sharp as an educator.

Every teacher can grow; reflection is how you choose the direction.

The best reflective moves share key traits:

- **Intentional** – Planned, not accidental. Build reflection into your routine.
- **Ongoing** – Part of your practice, not just when things go wrong.
- **Evidence-Based** – Grounded in student work, data, and observations.
- **Constructive** – Focused on action, not self-criticism.
- **Collaborative** – Invite feedback from students, colleagues, and mentors.

When reflection is a regular part of your practice, you turn everyday teaching into insight, and insight into stronger teaching. It's how good teachers become great ones—and how great teachers stay grounded, even in the most unpredictable moments.

Make time for it. Invite others into it. And trust that every small step forward matters.

Real Talk: What This Looks Like in Action

Your lesson on persuasive writing felt flat. Students were off-task, and *your* energy dipped too.

What do you do?

- You review the exit tickets and see most students didn't fully grasp the writing structure—***data-based reflection move.***
- You jot down a quick note in your planner: "Model structure earlier. Add examples."—***reflection journaling move.***
- You check in with a colleague to ask how they launch persuasive writing—***peer feedback move.***
- You adjust tomorrow's lesson to reframe the concept and build in more scaffolding—***action planning move.***
- Later in the week, you ask students how confident they feel in their writing—***student feedback move.***

That cycle of reflection, adjustment, and more reflection keeps you aligned with what students need and where you want to grow.

You can't change what you don't notice.

You Don't Have to Do It all at Once

Reflection doesn't need to be long or formal. It just needs to be consistent.

Start simple:

- Journal once a week about what's working and what's not.
- Use exit tickets weekly to check understanding and your teaching impact.

- Arrange one peer observation per term.
- Spend five minutes reviewing before planning your next lessons.

Small steps, done regularly, make the biggest difference.

Let's Explore: 7 Reflective Moves

On the following pages, we'll look at seven practical moves you can use to strengthen your instruction, deepen your awareness, and grow in your practice without adding more stress to your plate:

Exit Tickets
Student Feedback
Reflection Journaling
Success and Struggle Mapping
Peer Observation
Action Planning
Professional Learning Communities

Let's take a closer look at each.

Exit Tickets

Purpose:

To quickly assess student understanding, encourage reflection, and gather feedback to inform future instruction and teaching practices.

Description:

This strategy involves giving short prompts at the close of a lesson to check understanding, surface questions, and inform future instruction. An exit ticket provides a valuable snapshot of what students learned, what's unclear, and how ready they are to move forward.

How to Use It:

1. Pose a Prompt

Ask students to answer a question, summarize a key idea, reflect on their learning, or explain a concept in their own words:

- "What's one thing you learned today?"
- "What's one question you still have?"

2. Use Flexible Formats

Have students respond on sticky notes, index cards, slips of paper, or digitally through a classroom platform.

3. Collect Responses

Gather the exit tickets as students leave the classroom or before transitioning to the next activity.

4. Review and Reflect

Look for patterns.

- Who's ready to move on?
- Who needs more support?
- Which concepts may need reteaching?

5. **Plan Accordingly**

   Use the data to adjust your pacing, group students for targeted support, or plan a follow-up activity.

Example: At the end of a history lesson, you ask, "Write one thing you learned today and one question you still have." As students leave, they hand in their slips. You review them after class to identify misunderstandings and plan the next day's instruction.

When to Use It:

- At the end of any lesson or learning block
- When you need quick formative assessment data
- To encourage student reflection and self-assessment
- Before moving on to a new topic or skill

Why It Works:

✓ Provides real-time insight into student learning

✓ Supports responsive teaching and targeted reteaching

✓ Encourages student reflection and accountability

✓ Simple to implement with minimal prep

Student Feedback

Purpose:

To improve teaching practices and classroom climate by actively seeking and acting on student input.

Description:

This strategy involves collecting and acting on feedback from students to foster a culture of trust and collaboration. It helps you understand what's working, what needs adjusting, and how students experience learning. When students see their feedback led to change, they feel valued and more invested in the classroom.

How to Use It:

1. Create a Simple Feedback Tool

Develop short surveys, reflection prompts, or a suggestion box to gather input. Focus on specific areas such as teaching strategies, classroom routines, or content clarity.

2. Ask Targeted Questions

Use open-ended prompts to get meaningful responses:

- "What helps you learn best in this class?"
- "What's one thing we could change to make learning easier?"
- "Is there something we should keep doing because it works well?"

3. Collect and Review Responses

Look for patterns or repeated comments that highlight strengths and areas for growth.

4. Act on the Feedback

Make small, purposeful changes—adjust pacing, add movement breaks, or offer more participation options.

5. Close the Loop

Let students know how their feedback was used:

- "I noticed many of you wanted more partner work, so we'll add that into next week's lessons."

Example: You ask, "What helps you feel comfortable and ready to learn? What's one change that would make our classroom better?" Several students say the current seating makes it hard to see the board and collaborate. You rearrange desks into small groups with some individual seats (for students who prefer that), then tell the class, "Your feedback helped me make this change so we can work together more easily."

When to Use It:

- After trying a new teaching method
- Midway through a unit or term
- Periodically throughout the year to check the classroom climate
- When classroom dynamics shift

Why It Works:

✓ Builds trust and respect between teacher and students

✓ Encourages student ownership in the learning environment

✓ Provides insight for responsive, targeted adjustments

✓ Supports continuous improvement for both teaching and learning

Reflection Journaling

Purpose:

To strengthen teaching practice by recording and reflecting on classroom experiences, student interactions, and instructional decisions.

Description:

This strategy involves using a structured method to pause, process, and learn from your daily work. By writing regularly about your successes, challenges, and student responses, you build awareness of your practice, track growth over time, and make more intentional instructional choices.

How to Use It:

1. **Set a Routine**

   Choose a consistent time to reflect—after lessons, at the end of the week, or following significant classroom moments.

2. **Focus Your Entries**

   Write about what went well, what challenges came up, and how students engaged with your strategies.

3. **Use Reflective Questions**

   Guide your thinking with questions like:

   - "What did I do today that supported student learning?"
   - "What surprised me in student responses?"
   - "What would I change if I taught this lesson again?"

4. **Track Growth**

   Review past entries periodically to notice patterns, celebrate progress, and identify ongoing areas for improvement.

5. **Use for Planning**

   Let your reflections shape your next steps in instruction, classroom management, and professional development goals.

Example: After a group activity, you might write: "The group work was more chaotic than I expected. Next time, I'll assign clearer roles and model how to share ideas respectfully. Once I clarified expectations midway, the noise level dropped and focus improved." This reflection informs adjustments for future lessons and strengthens classroom routines.

When to Use It:

- After lessons or review sessions
- Following successes, challenges, or breakthroughs worth learning from
- Anytime you want to grow your awareness and refine your teaching

Why It Works:

✓ Encourages intentional reflection and growth
✓ Helps identify patterns and track progress
✓ Improves instructional decision-making
✓ Builds habits of continuous professional learning

Success and Struggle Mapping

Purpose:

To identify strengths, challenges, and next steps by reflecting on what worked and what didn't in a lesson, unit, or week.

Description:

This strategy involves a simple reflective practice where you capture both wins and challenges after teaching. By recording these moments consistently, you can identify patterns, celebrate growth, and make targeted adjustments to improve instruction and classroom management.

How to Use It:

1. Pause and Reflect

After a lesson or day, jot down:

- One *success* (for example, what clicked, where students thrived)
- One *struggle* (for example, a dip in engagement, confusion with content, or a management challenge)

2. Be Specific

Go beyond "It went well" by naming *why*.

3. Look for Patterns Over Time

Review notes weekly or monthly to notice trends. Are certain strategies consistently working? Are specific areas repeatedly challenging?

4. Plan for Action

Reinforce what's working and create a plan for addressing struggles—reteach, adjust pacing, or try a new approach.

5. Celebrate Growth

Reflect on how your teaching is evolving. This practice highlights improvements, not just challenges. Be sure to acknowledge the wins.

Example: After a science unit, you reflect:

- **Success:** Inquiry-based group work kept students highly engaged during experiments.
- **Struggle:** Students struggled to write detailed lab reports. Next time, model the writing process more explicitly and use sentence starters.

When to Use It:

- At the end of lessons, weeks, or units
- During planning sessions or team reflections
- Anytime you want to refine your practice with concrete insights

Why It Works:

✓ Highlights both strengths and areas for growth

✓ Turns reflection into actionable next steps

✓ Helps identify long-term trends in teaching practice

✓ Encourages a growth mindset

Peer Observation

Purpose:

To learn from colleagues' teaching practices to spark new ideas, refine your own strategies, and build a culture of professional growth.

Description:

This strategy involves observing a colleague in action to provide fresh insights into teaching methods, classroom management, and student engagement. By reflecting on what you see, you can strengthen your own practice while fostering collaboration and trust among peers.

How to Use It:

1. **Plan the Observation**

   Coordinate with a colleague and agree on a focus area, such as questioning strategies, pacing, differentiation, or student engagement.

2. **Observe with Intention**

   Take focused notes during the lesson. Record specific teacher moves, student reactions, and techniques that stand out. Capture both strategies to try and moments that prompt reflection.

3. **Debrief and Discuss**

   Meet after the lesson to share observations, ask questions, and discuss how strategies could be adapted for your classroom.

4. **Apply What You Learn**

   Choose at least one idea to implement in your own teaching. Reflect afterward on its impact and consider sharing results with your colleague.

5. **Keep It Reciprocal**

   Offer to host your own lesson for observation to promote shared learning and professional reciprocity.

Example: You observe a colleague teaching a math lesson and notice how they scaffold complex problems by asking guiding questions instead of giving direct answers. In reflecting, you realize you often jump in too quickly and decide to use more open-ended questioning in your own lessons to foster student critical thinking and problem-solving.

When to Use It:

- During professional learning cycles
- As part of school initiatives
- Regularly (monthly or quarterly)
- When seeking inspiration, feedback, or support with specific instructional challenges

Why It Works:

✓ Provides real, practical examples of teaching in action

✓ Strengthens collaboration and trust between colleagues

✓ Encourages reflection and professional growth

✓ Brings fresh perspectives into your classroom

Action Planning

Purpose:

To turn reflection and feedback into concrete steps for growth.

Description:

This strategy involves turning insights from reflection or feedback into a structured plan for growth. It bridges the gap between insight and implementation by setting clear goals and outlining how you'll achieve them.

How to Use It:

1. **Identify a Focus Area**

   After reflecting or receiving feedback, choose one or two areas you want to strengthen.

2. **Set Specific Goals**

   Write goals that are realistic, measurable, and tied to student learning or classroom practice. Include both short-term and long-term targets.

3. **Break Goals into Steps**

   List practical actions you can take—such as testing strategies, exploring resources, or collaborating with colleagues.

4. **Set a Timeline**

   Decide when you'll implement each step and schedule regular check-ins to track progress.

5. **Review and Adjust**

   Reflect on what's working, refine your plan as needed, and celebrate growth along the way.

Example: After noticing small group instruction isn't as effective as you'd like, you create an action plan to strengthen guided reading. Your plan includes:

- Reading a professional article on managing multiple reading groups
- Creating a revised schedule to maximize time with each group
- Designing comprehension questions for upcoming texts in advance
- Meeting with your literacy coach in two weeks to reflect and discuss

This structured plan keeps your focus clear and ensures ongoing progress.

When to Use It:

- Following a challenging lesson
- In response to student feedback
- After a peer observation
- During professional learning cycles
- As part of goal-setting or coaching conversations

Why It Works:

✓ Moves reflection from "insight" to "implementation"

✓ Keeps professional growth intentional and measurable

✓ Provides accountability and structure

✓ Builds momentum through small, achievable steps

Professional Learning Communities

Purpose:

To foster collaboration among teachers to improve teaching practices and student outcomes.

Description:

This strategy involves engaging in regular collaboration with other teachers to reflect on teaching practices, share strategies, and analyze student learning. PLCs provide a structured way for you to grow together, solve challenges, and continuously improve instruction.

How to Use It:

1. Meet with Intention

Set a regular meeting time with your grade-level team, subject team, or cross-grade colleagues. Begin with a clear focus—such as analyzing student writing, improving questioning strategies, or addressing behavior challenges.

2. Examine Student Work and Data

Bring assessments, work samples, or observation notes. Discuss where students excel and where they struggle. Use these insights to guide instructional decisions.

3. Share Strategies and Try New Approaches

Exchange teaching practices and classroom moves. Agree to test at least one new strategy before the next meeting, then share outcomes.

4. Reflect with Guiding Questions

Use prompts like:

- What strategies are helping students most?
- Where are we noticing consistent challenges?
- How can we adjust instruction to better meet student needs?

5. **Document and Plan Next Steps**

   Keep notes, set clear action steps, and hold each other accountable in a supportive way.

Example: As part of the grade 7 PLC, you meet every two weeks with your grade-level team to review student writing samples. Collectively, you notice many students struggle with organizing ideas. The team decides to use the same graphic organizer across classrooms. At the next meeting, you'll review new samples, share successes, and refine your approach.

When to Use It:

- Throughout the school year
- When launching new units
- When analyzing student progress
- When tackling persistent challenges

Why It Works:

✓ Breaks down teacher isolation

✓ Encourages collaboration and accountability

✓ Improves student outcomes through shared problem-solving

✓ Builds a supportive, growth-oriented school culture

Final Thoughts

Reflective moves are how you stay connected to your purpose, refine your practice, and ensure your teaching evolves with your students.

The most effective teachers aren't the ones who have all the answers. They're the ones who keep asking questions—what worked? what didn't? what can I try next? Curiosity fuels growth.

And here's the beauty of reflection: it doesn't need to be big or time-consuming. A quick note, a student check-in, a five-minute chat with a colleague—these small moments build a habit of continuous learning.

Over time, reflective moves shift your mindset. You stop chasing perfect lessons and start building purposeful ones. You become more confident, more adaptable, and more connected to the work that matters.

So, keep checking in with yourself. Keep adjusting. Keep learning. The more you grow, the more your students do too.

And that's the kind of impact that lasts.

Up Next

As we close our look at reflective moves, remember that none of these strategies happen in isolation—they grow best in a classroom that's been thoughtfully prepared for them.

Our final chapter brings everything full circle, focusing on the foundational work that makes all these moves possible. From how you arrange your space to how you structure your routines, these behind-the-scenes decisions create the conditions in which all the moves you've explored can truly thrive.

Before the first lesson even begins, the way you set the stage determines how every move will land.

Let's explore how to lay that foundation.

PUTTING IT INTO PRACTICE

Now that you've seen the why and how behind effective reflective moves, let's explore what they might look like in real life.

The following scenarios are pulled from common classroom moments—ones that every teacher has faced in some form. Each one invites you to pause, reflect, and consider:

What moves might I make in this moment?

This is where theory meets practice—and where your instincts and toolkit come together.

SCENARIOS

The Noisy, Wiggly Day (Again)

The Lesson That Didn't Land

Chaos in the Gym

Scenario 1: The Noisy, Wiggly Day (Again)

It's mid-October in your grade 1 classroom, and lately, every day has started to feel the same.

You gather students on the carpet for your morning meeting, but within minutes:

- Tatum is rolling on the floor.
- Willow keeps interrupting to tell you about her cat.
- Rowan and Asher are whispering and poking each other.
- You remind them (again) to sit "criss-cross, hands in your lap," but it barely lasts a minute.

By the time you finish calendar and weather, you feel exhausted. It's only 9:15 am.

Transitions are messy. Noise levels climb quickly. Even your most patient students are starting to act out. You've tried attention signals, proximity, and positive reinforcement, but the behaviors continue.

At the end of the day, you sit at your desk and think:

- Is it them or is it me?
- Have I been consistent enough? Clear enough?
- Am I expecting too much for this age or not structuring things enough?

You care deeply about your students. But right now, your classroom feels more reactive than responsive.

You know it's time to pause. To reflect.

How Might You Respond?

- What reflective moves could help you evaluate your classroom management routines and expectations?
- How might you involve students in resetting classroom norms and building shared responsibility?
- What small, intentional changes could have a big impact on behaviour and learning?

Scenario 2: The Lesson That Didn't Land

It's the end of the day in your grade 5 classroom, and students have just packed up their things. The room is finally quiet, and you sit for a moment, replaying the afternoon's math lesson in your head.

You had planned what you thought was a strong, hands-on activity about fractions. It included manipulatives, visual models, and partner discussion.

But in real time, things didn't go the way you'd hoped.

- Students were confused from the start.
- Several kept asking the same clarifying question, and you found yourself repeating instructions.
- A few students started acting out halfway through.
- Lydia left the group in tears after her partner called her answer "dumb."
- And when you checked the exit tickets...more than half the class missed the concept.

Now, sitting alone at your desk, you feel frustrated. Tired. Disappointed.

You wonder:

- Was the lesson too complex?
- Did I miss an opportunity to pre-teach something?
- Should I have paused sooner when I noticed confusion?

You know moments like this are part of teaching. But still, you want to do better.

How Might You Respond?

- What reflective moves could help you analyze what didn't work and why?
- How might you use this experience to refine tomorrow's plan or revisit the concept?
- How can you balance self-compassion with professional growth in moments like this?

Scenario 3: Chaos in the Gym

It's Wednesday afternoon, and your grade 4 class has gym. You've planned a fast-paced circuit of fitness stations—jump rope, push-ups, relay cones, balance boards, and squats. The goal is to build stamina and teamwork while keeping everyone active.

You model the stations, explain the rotation, assign partners, and send them off.

Within minutes, things start to unravel:

- Two students argue about whose turn it is at the cones.
- One group skips a station completely and runs laps instead.
- Several students are standing around, waiting for you to tell them what to do.
- A few are horsing around and using equipment incorrectly.
- And Addison, who usually loves gym, is standing on the sidelines, arms crossed, clearly disengaged.

You blow the whistle and regroup the class, frustrated.

"Why aren't we following directions?" you ask.

A few students shrug. One says, "We didn't know where to go next."

You finish the class, but something doesn't sit right. Back in the classroom, you pause to reflect:

- Did I give too many instructions at once?
- Did students understand the expectations?
- Were the stations inclusive and accessible for all learners?

You realize it's not just about behavior. It's about structure, clarity, and meeting students where they are.

How Might You Respond?

- What reflective moves could help you identify where your lesson design or delivery might need adjustment?
- How can you better support students in understanding, following, and engaging with the activity?
- What could you do differently next time to make gym more structured, inclusive, and successful?

Chapter 10
Laying the Foundation

"Being in this class makes me want to come to school." —**Grade 8 student**

Why Foundations Matter

At this point, you've collected ninety-eight teacher moves—small, powerful actions that can shift a lesson, re-engage a student, or change the tone of the classroom. These moves are about reading the room, responding in real time, and creating space for meaningful learning.

But even the sharpest moves can fall flat if they're built on shaky ground. Just like you wouldn't start building a house before leveling the land and pouring the foundation, you can't expect your best strategies to work in a chaotic, unclear, or unprepared environment.

The quiet work you do *before* students arrive—designing the space, shaping routines, and setting the schedule—determines how every move will land. That's what this chapter is about: the unseen groundwork that makes great teaching possible.

Here are eight steps to set you up for success.

Step 1: Know Your Students

Before a single bulletin board goes up or a desk is moved into place, there's one essential step that too often gets skipped: really looking at *who* you're teaching.

Your students aren't just a list of names; they're a diverse group of learners with stories, needs, preferences, and personalities. And before you set up the space they'll spend their days in, it's worth spending some quiet time getting to know them.

Start with the basics. Pull out your class list, pour a coffee, and begin asking the kinds of questions that help you prepare with intention:

- Do any students require accommodations or assistive technology?
- Do any students receive support from other professionals at school?
- Are there students who might benefit from alternative seating, movement breaks or access to a calming space?
- Do any students need proximity to me for focus or support?
- Are there individual education plans, safety plans, or medical reports I need to review?

As you work through these—and other questions—make notes or create a chart to guide your decisions. Not just now, but throughout the school year. This is also a great opportunity to begin your documentation file for each student.

This isn't just logistics—it's equity and inclusion in action. You're designing a classroom for *your learners*, not just "a" class.

A classroom's culture is built in the quiet, unseen work you do before the year begins.

Step 2: Know Yourself

Once you've got a sense of your learners' needs, shift your focus inward. What are your own preferences as a teacher? What do *you* need to feel grounded and effective?

Ask yourself questions like:

- What do I need to teach well?
- How do I want my classroom to feel?
- What makes my classroom comfortable for me?
- What space do I need for myself?

Your teaching assignment and style matter just as much as the student profile when designing a space and schedule that will work.

Then, zoom out. Take stock of any barriers or structural limitations you'll need to work around:

- Am I sharing a room with another teacher or support staff member?
- Is the space unusually small or especially large?
- Am I teaching in a portable?
- Do my students have lockers, or will backpacks stay in the room?
- Am I short on storage, wall space, or furniture?

Naming the obstacles early helps you avoid frustration later. It also gives you a clearer picture of what's within your control and what isn't.

Finally, give yourself permission to dream. If you could design your ideal classroom from scratch, what would it look like, sound like, and feel like? Write it down. Even if you can't have everything on your wish list, it will guide your choices, help you advocate for what matters, and remind you of the kind of space you want to create.

When you really know who you're teaching—and what you need to teach well—you don't just set up a classroom. You create a space with purpose.

Step 3: Design Your Space with Purpose

Once you've taken time to really understand your learners, reflect on your teaching preferences, and get honest about the space you're working with, it's time to roll up your sleeves and set the stage.

Your classroom isn't just a room. It's a living, breathing environment. It influences how your students feel the moment they walk in—whether they feel calm or overstimulated, confident or unsure. It tells them what's possible, what's expected, and whether they belong.

Before you start decorating or moving furniture, walk through these steps:

Declutter

Start with the part that no one loves, but everyone benefits from: decluttering. Yes—even that shelf in the corner and especially that bin you haven't opened in three years.

Go through everything and ask yourself:

- Have I used this in the last year?
- Does this still reflect how I teach?
- Does this serve my students, or is it just taking up space?

If the answer is no, let it go.

Old resources, broken baskets, and stacks of outdated worksheets aren't helping you teach better. They're just taking up oxygen.

Make room for what matters. Your classroom should feel like possibility, not pressure.

Take Stock

Now that you've cleared some space, it's time to see what's left: what do you have to work with?

Think in categories:

- Student desks and seating

- Group tables or workstations
- Carpet areas, calming corners, classroom library
- Teacher desk and resources
- Student materials
- Shelves, cubbies, bins
- Technology
- Display space (for charts, visuals, student work)

If you're holding onto something but can't name how you'll use it, that's your sign to let it go.

Gather What You Need

Once you've taken stock, you'll likely have a list of things you need. Before heading to your favorite dollar store or falling down a Pinterest rabbit hole—pause. You likely have access to more than you think.

Try this first:

- Ask your grade team or colleagues if they have extras
- Check your school's storage or supply room
- Chat with your custodial team (they often know where hidden gems are)
- Reach out to administration for key materials, especially curriculum-related ones
- Ask family or friends if they have small items (shelves, rugs, stools) they no longer need

But here's the golden rule: **Only bring in what serves a clear purpose.**

You just decluttered—don't refill your room with things that don't directly support your teaching or student learning.

Map It Out

Before moving desks or filling bins, sketch your space on paper. Start with what can't be moved—doors, windows, sinks, electrical outlets, whiteboards, built-in shelves.

Then layer in the big pieces:

- Desks or tables
- Group work areas
- Carpet or gathering spaces
- Teacher space and resources
- Book bins, manipulatives, or student materials

Ask yourself:

- Is there a natural flow for movement?
- Does the setup make logistical sense?
- Are pathways clear and accessible?
- Have I considered individual student needs?
- Can students easily access materials when needed?
- Is there a balance of quiet and collaborative zones?
- Does everything have a place?

Now, imagine a full school day in that space: morning entry, learning centers, math lesson on the carpet, a science experiment, lining up for recess, lunch. Does the setup support the rhythm of your day?

If it works on paper, it's worth trying. If something feels off even before the furniture moves, adjust now, not later. This is your classroom's backstage, and the choices you make here shape how everything else unfolds.

When your physical space reflects your values—organization, inclusion, calm, flexibility—your students notice. Even if they can't name it, they'll feel it. And you'll feel more confident, grounded, and ready to lead.

A calm, organized space is an open invitation to learn.

Step 4: Build a Schedule That Works for You and Them

Planning your class schedule typically begins with receiving your timetable at the school level from your principal. This master timetable reflects the larger puzzle of staffing, space, and contractual obligations. It's important to understand what's non-negotiable—prep periods, specialist classes, support times—but also to:

- Ask questions about things that don't make sense.
- Flag scheduling issues that conflict with student needs.
- Be a respectful advocate when adjustments may be needed.

Once your school-level timetable is set, you can focus on your class's daily schedule.

Here are some things to consider:

- The transitions required between subjects or blocks of time.
- Student energy levels and focus during different points in the day.
- Following high-energy periods (like recess or PE) with calm activities.
- Scheduling prep-heavy lessons (like visual arts) after breaks for easier setup.

- Individual student needs and support schedules.
- Consistent blocks for literacy and math.

Your schedule is your blueprint. It won't be perfect, but it can be intentional. Once you feel confident with it, live with it for a few weeks and then adjust as needed.

Step 5: Structure Your Learning Blocks

Structuring your learning blocks is about bringing clarity and rhythm to each subject you teach. While every subject has its own demands, the goal is the same: to break time into intentional segments that support instruction, practice, and reflection.

Whether you're teaching math, literacy, science, or the arts, each block should have a beginning, middle, and end—a clear opening to activate thinking, a core period for skill-building or exploration, and time to consolidate learning before moving on.

This structure gives students a predictable flow they can settle into, while giving you a flexible framework for planning. It also creates space for formative assessment, targeted support, and deeper engagement—without the chaos of trying to "wing it" from one activity to the next.

The more consistent your structure, the easier it becomes to manage time, maintain focus, and maximize impact across the day.

Structure builds predictability.

Predictability builds safety.

And safety builds engagement.

Step 6: Intentionally Develop Your Routines

If there's one thing that holds a classroom together, it's consistent routines.

Routines are the invisible framework that reduce anxiety, promote independence, and free up your time and energy for actual teaching—not constant managing. When students know what to expect, they can focus on learning instead of trying to figure out what's happening next.

Start by walking through your day, step by step. Think like a student. Where do I put my backpack? What do I do when I finish my work? How do I get help without disrupting the class? Every moment that feels obvious to you as the teacher might feel confusing to a student unless it's clearly taught.

These are some key routines to plan and explicitly teach:

- **Morning entry**: What do students do as soon as they walk in? Do they hang up their bags, hand in homework, start an activity?
- **Accessing and returning supplies:** How do they get what they need independently? Where do materials go when finished?

- **Transitions between subjects or rooms:** What does a smooth shift look like?
- **Asking for help:** When and how can they get support without disrupting others?
- **Early finishers:** What do they do if they have extra time after completing a task?
- **Noise levels:** What's the expected volume for different activities?
- **End-of-day dismissal:** How do they pack up and get ready to go home?

During the first few weeks, these routines ***are*** the curriculum. Teach them like you would a lesson: model, practice, give feedback, and try again. Use visual cues, verbal prompts, and consistent positive reinforcement. It may feel repetitive, but it pays off.

Once students know the routines, you'll be amazed how much more you can do. Your classroom will run with calm, clarity, and confidence—because everyone understands the expectations.

Strong routines build independence.

Step 7: Master Your Transitions

Transitions are often overlooked, and yet they happen constantly: moving from one subject to the next, heading to assemblies or special events, returning from recess, gathering on the carpet, or lining up for dismissal. These mini moments can either keep your classroom flowing or cause it to unravel.

The key is to plan for transitions as intentionally as you plan your lessons.

Start by mapping them out. Consider everything:

- Subject to subject
- Room to room
- Whole class to independent work time, small group, or learning stations
- Structured to unstructured time
- Re-entry from recess, lunch, library, or gym
- Switching between teachers or support staff
- Different components of the same subject block
- Movement breaks

Build in realistic buffer time. Not every transition needs to be lightning-fast. In fact, rushing often causes more harm than good. Instead, plan a minute or two for students to reset, gather materials, and refocus their energy.

Use simple tools to make transitions smoother:

- Music to signal a change
- A countdown timer or visual clock
- A consistent verbal cue or callback

Celebrate the smooth ones. Acknowledge what went well and why it worked. And when a transition doesn't go as planned, don't ignore it—reteach it. Use it as a learning opportunity.

Time lost to messy transitions isn't just about minutes; it's about momentum, attention, and tone. Calm, clear, and consistent transitions make your day more manageable and your students more secure.

Plan for them. Practice them. Be intentional.

Step 8: Make the First Two Weeks Count

If you're feeling the pressure to dive headfirst into the curriculum, take a deep breath and pause.

The first two weeks are not about content—they're about community.

These early days set the tone for your learning environment. If your classroom isn't a community first, even the strongest lessons won't matter.

Use the first two weeks to:

- Learn your students, and let them learn you.
- Co-create classroom agreements.
- Teach and practice routines.
- Model kindness and respect.
- Create a space where every student feels they belong.

This doesn't always show up in a lesson plan, but it is some of the most important teaching you'll ever do.

Classroom culture isn't built by hanging a motivational poster. It's built through consistent expectations, calm redirections, warm greetings, silly moments, and daily reminders that we're in this together. It's built through how you show up—every day—for them.

Give yourself permission to slow down and get the community right. The curriculum will follow. When students feel like they belong, everything else—engagement, effort, growth—gets a little easier.

Make these two weeks count. They're the foundation your entire year will stand on.

Final Thoughts

The moves you've learned—classroom management, instructional, relationship-building, engagement, differentiation, adaptive, emotional support, reflective—only work because *you* do the quiet groundwork first. You design the space. You build the routines. You create the culture.

Before the first anchor chart goes up or the first group project begins, you've already shaped how the year will feel. Not with perfection, but with presence and intention.

They work because of *you.*

Be Great!

The best teachers don't rely on tricks or trends. They rely on clarity, consistency, and care. That's what this chapter—and this book—is really about.

Always remember:

You don't have to be perfect.
You don't need all the answers.
You will have messy moments.
You will adjust.
You will grow.

And between the chaos and the calm, the breakthroughs and the re-dos, the quiet wins and the loud ones—*you will make an impact.*

Start strong.
Be intentional.
Trust your instincts.
Keep showing up.
You've got the moves.
You've got the heart.
You've got the power to make this year
unforgettable—for your students, and for yourself.
You're ready.
Go be great!

Quick Reference Guide

98 High-Impact Strategies for Better Teaching and Learning Outcomes

Classroom Management Moves

Structured Routines ... 15
Daily Schedule ... 17
Strategic Seating ... 19
The Proximity Effect ... 21
Nonverbal Cues ... 23
Attention Signals ... 25
Name-Dropping ... 27
Positive Narration ... 29
Wait-and-Redirect ... 31
Noise Level Chart ... 33
Structured Choice ... 35
Front-Loading Expectations ... 37
Transition Timers ... 39
Movement Breaks ... 41

Instructional Moves

Activating Prior Knowledge ... 55
Questioning ... 57
Wait Time ... 59
Think-Pair-Share ... 61
Modeling ... 63
Scaffolding ... 65
Chunking ... 67
Spiraling ... 69
Checking for Understanding ... 71
Error Analysis ... 73
Anchor Charts ... 75
Visuals ... 77
Multisensory Approach ... 79
Multiple Modalities ... 81
Metacognition ... 83

Relationship-Building Moves

Greeting at the Door 97
Using Student Names 99
Incorporating Student Interests 101
Sharing About Yourself 103
Active Listening 105
Using Humor 107
Positive Reinforcement 109
"What's Working" Conversations 111
Highlighting Strengths 113
Celebrating Successes 115
Two-by-Ten Strategy 117
Restorative Circles 119
Community Circle 121

Engagement Moves

Callbacks and Chants 135
Building Anticipation 137
Reading Aloud 139
Student-Led Learning 141
Peer Collaboration 143
Class Debates 145
Cold Calling 147
Hands-On Activities 149
Gamification 151
Real-World Connections 153
Problem-Based Learning 155
Technology and Interactive Media 157

Differentiation Moves

Timely Feedback 171
Small Group Instruction 173
Scaffolded Writing Prompts 175
Parallel Tasks 177
Tiered Tasks 179
Curriculum Compacting 181
Flexible Grouping 183
Learning Stations 185
Choice Boards 187
Learning Menus 189
Student Experts 191

Checklists 193
Differentiated Rubrics 195
Multiple Means of Assessment 197
Enrichment Opportunities 199
Goal Setting 201

Adaptive Moves

Adjusting Pacing 215
Offering Multiple Explanations 217
Responding to Student Questioning 219
Circling Back 221
Stop and Reset 223
Reframing the Task 225
Task Reduction 227

Emotional Support Moves

Creating a Safe Space 239
Mindfulness Practices 241
Daily Affirmations 243
Practicing Gratitude 245
Emotional Labeling 247
Self-Regulation Tools 249
Acknowledging Effort 251
Normalizing Mistakes 253
Celebrating Small Wins 255
Private Check-Ins 257
Empathy Statements 259
Empowering Language 261
Good News Visits 263
Positive Communication Home 265

Reflective Moves

Exit Tickets 279
Student Feedback 281
Reflection Journaling 283
Success and Struggle Mapping 285
Peer Observation 287
Action Planning 289
Professional Learning Communities 291

About the Author

Shannon Hazel spent twenty-five years as a teacher, special education specialist, instructional coach, and AQ course instructor. She knows firsthand the realities of today's classrooms and the challenges educators face in meeting the diverse needs of students.

Passionate about supporting and celebrating teachers, Shannon is on a mission to empower new teachers and advocate for systemic change in public education. Her first book, *New Teacher Confidential: What They Didn't Tell You* about Being a Teacher, has become a trusted resource in teacher training programs and is widely shared by teachers' unions to support graduates and early-career teachers alike. Shannon also enjoys speaking to new teachers and leading workshops inspired by her books.

In 2023, Shannon was honored with the Educator Award from the Council for Exceptional Children in recognition of her leadership and advocacy for students with special needs.

She lives in Ontario, Canada, with her two children and her dog, Rosco. Now enjoying life after the classroom, Shannon continues her work as an author, mentor, and advocate dedicated to uplifting teachers.

Also by Shannon Hazel

New Teacher Confidential:
What They Didn't Tell You about Being a Teacher

What every new teacher really needs to know.

Grab a Copy!

www.ingramcontent.com/pod-product-compliance
Lightning Source LLC
Chambersburg PA
CBHW081423090426
42740CB00017B/3159

* 9 7 8 1 7 3 8 2 5 9 3 2 8 *